BEWARE THE WATCHFUL EYE

OF THOSE WHO CAN SEE THROUGH THE ARTFUL LIE.

FOR INTELLIGENCE, KEEN AND BRIGHT,

WILL PIERCE THE DARKNESS WITH ITS LIGHT.

INSTRUCTIONS

Read and reflect on each section. Then, choose one or more of the reflection prompts to fill in the journal page. There are additional journal pages in the back. Use the index to easily reference the topics/areas reflected upon. The author also has blank journals available for sale.

TABLE OF CONTENTS

ABOUT BALTASAR GRACIÁN

Baltasar Gracián, a renowned Spanish Jesuit and Baroque prose writer, was born on January 8, 1601, in Belmonte de Calatayud, Spain. His life was marked by a dedication to scholarship and a profound understanding of human nature, reflected in his literary works that continue to inspire readers worldwide.

Gracián's early years were shaped by his education at the Jesuit school in Zaragoza, where he exhibited remarkable intellectual prowess. He later joined the Society of Jesus in 1619, embracing a life of religious devotion and scholarship. His keen intellect and dedication to learning led him to pursue further studies in philosophy and theology at the University of Zaragoza, where he excelled in his academic pursuits.

During his time as a Jesuit, Gracián held various teaching positions, imparting knowledge to students while deepening his understanding of human psychology and morality. His experiences within the Jesuit order gave him insights into the complexities of human relationships and the challenges of navigating his time's social and political landscapes.

Gracián's literary career flourished with the publication of his seminal work, "El Criticón," a three-part allegorical novel that explores themes of wisdom, morality, and the human condition. This intricate and philosophical work established him as one of the leading figures of Spanish Baroque literature. His writing style - wit, moral depth, and profound observations of human behavior - earned him acclaim and recognition as a master of Spanish prose.

In addition to "El Criticón," Gracián authored several other influential works, including "The Art of Worldly Wisdom" ("El Arte de la Prudencia"), a collection of aphorisms and reflections on life, ethics, and success. This timeless masterpiece continues to be celebrated for its practical wisdom and insightful guidance on navigating the complexities of existence.

Baltasar Gracián passed away on December 6, 1658, leaving behind a rich legacy of literature that continues to captivate and enlighten readers worldwide.

ABOUT NICCOLÒ MACHIAVELLI

Niccolò Machiavelli, born on May 3, 1469, in Florence, Italy, was a prominent figure of the Italian Renaissance and a versatile writer, diplomat, and philosopher. Little is known about his early life, but he received a humanist education, which laid the foundation for his future career.

Machiavelli entered the public service of the Florentine Republic in 1494, during a period of political turmoil in Italy. He held various government positions, including secretary of the Second Chancery, where he gained firsthand experience in diplomacy and statecraft. His exposure to the intricacies of political power and the volatile nature of Italian politics greatly influenced his later works.

In 1513, Machiavelli wrote his most famous work, "The Prince," a political treatise exploring effective leadership and governance principles. The book is known for its pragmatic approach to politics, advocating for using cunning and manipulation to maintain power. Despite its controversial reputation, "The Prince" remains a seminal work in political theory and has sparked widespread debate over Machiavelli's intentions and beliefs.

Following the fall of the Florentine Republic in 1512, Machiavelli's political career suffered a setback, and he was briefly imprisoned and tortured on suspicion of conspiracy. After his release, he retired to his estate outside Florence, where he devoted himself to writing and intellectual pursuits.

In addition to "The Prince," Machiavelli authored several other notable works, including "Discourses on Livy," "The Art of War," and "The History of Florence." These writings cover various topics, from military strategy to historical analysis, and reflect Machiavelli's deep understanding of human nature and politics.

Machiavelli died in Florence on June 21, 1527, leaving a complex and controversial legacy. Despite enduring criticism for his perceived amorality and Machiavellian tactics, his works continue to be studied and debated by scholars and politicians worldwide, cementing his status as one of the most influential figures in Western political thought.

WHY MACHIAVELLI?

In the modern era, the popularity of Niccolò Machiavelli's ideas has endured and continues to resonate. Firstly, Machiavelli's insights into politics and power remain relevant in contemporary society. His pragmatic approach to understanding human behavior and power dynamics has found

application in various fields, including politics, business, and international relations. Many of his concepts, such as the importance of adaptability and the necessity of making tough decisions for the greater good, continue to be studied and debated by scholars and practitioners alike.

Secondly, Machiavelli's writings continue to provoke thought and stimulate discussion. His works, particularly "The Prince" and "The Discourses on Livy," offer a wealth of ideas and observations open to interpretation and analysis. The complexity and ambiguity of Machiavelli's ideas allow for multiple perspectives and interpretations, making his writings a rich source of inspiration for scholars, philosophers, and students of politics.

Furthermore, Machiavelli's reputation as a controversial figure adds to his enduring popularity. His willingness to challenge conventional wisdom and unapologetic advocacy of pragmatism and realpolitik have earned him admirers and critics. Machiavelli's name has become

synonymous with cunning, manipulation, and amorality, yet his ideas spark fascination and intrigue.

Lastly, the influence of Machiavelli's ideas can be seen in popular culture, where his name and concepts are often referenced in books, movies, and television shows. From political dramas to business strategy guides, the Machiavellian ethos has permeated popular culture, further cementing his place in the modern imagination.

Thus, the enduring popularity of Machiavelli can be attributed to the timeless relevance of his ideas, the richness of his writings, his controversial reputation, and his pervasive influence on popular culture. As long as power dynamics and human behavior remain central to human society, Machiavelli's insights will continue to be studied, debated, and applied in various contexts.

THE USEFULNESS OF *THE ART OF WISDOM*

Baltasar Gracián's "The Art of Worldly Wisdom" is a masterpiece of

practical wisdom that offers

invaluable insights into navigating

the complexities of life with skill,

cunning, and strategic thinking.

Accordingly, the Machiavellian

interpretation of the usefulness of

The Art of Wisdom is inherently

pragmatic, emphasizing the

strategic deployment of intellect

and cunning to achieve political objectives. As understood via Niccolò

Machiavelli's seminal work, "The Prince," and his broader philosophy,

wisdom is not merely a virtue to be admired but a tool to be wielded in

pursuing and maintaining power.

To begin, "The Art of Worldly Wisdom" is essentially a manual for those

seeking to master the art of living. Gracián emphasizes the importance of

self-awareness, urging readers to understand their strengths, weaknesses,

and desires deeply. By knowing oneself, one can better navigate the

complexities of human relationships and make informed decisions that

align with their goals and values. As such, it furthers Machiavelli's central philosophy that rulers must possess a keen understanding of human nature to strategize effectively. For instance, one of the critical themes in Gracián's work is the importance of strategic thinking. He emphasizes the need to anticipate obstacles and plan actions accordingly, urging readers to adopt a flexible and adaptable mindset. In this context, wisdom is not confined to intellectual prowess or moral virtue. Still, it encompasses an intelligent understanding of power dynamics and the ability to utilize them to one's advantage.

Next, Like Machiavelli, Gracián also explores the art of persuasion, and he offers insights into influencing others and winning their trust and admiration. Both emphasize the importance of charm, wit, and charisma in interpersonal interactions, urging readers to cultivate these qualities to enhance their social standing and influence. These teachings on persuasion are particularly relevant in today's interconnected world, where networking and relationship-building are essential skills for success in both personal and professional spheres.

Further, Machiavelli emphasized the importance of managing alliances and relationships. Rulers must be astute judges of character and recognize when to cultivate

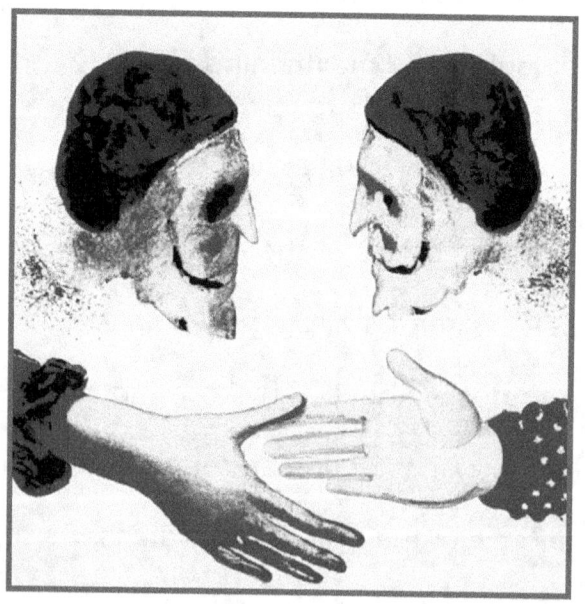

friendships and when to neutralize threats. "The Art of Worldly Wisdom" offers valuable insights into the nature of human relationships. Gracián's work explores power, loyalty, and betrayal dynamics, offering advice on navigating the complexities of interpersonal interactions with

grace and poise. He emphasizes the importance of trust and integrity in building lasting relationships while acknowledging the need for caution and discretion in dealing with potential adversaries.

In addition, while Machiavelli acknowledged the necessity of deception and manipulation in politics, he also recognized the importance of virtù (i.e., virtuous leadership) in securing long-term stability and success. Wise rulers must strike a delicate balance between pragmatism and morality, using their wisdom not only to attain power but also to govern wisely and justly for the benefit of their subjects. Since Gracián's religious background promotes virtuous living, it likewise promotes virtù. To conclude, the Machiavellian interpretation of the usefulness of *The Art of Wisdom* is multifaceted, encompassing both practical and strategic considerations.

1 - EVERYTHING IS AT ITS ACME

Everything is at its acme, especially the art of making one's way in the world. More is required nowadays to make a single wise man than formerly to make Seven Sages, and more is needed nowadays to deal with a single person than was required with a whole people in former times.

The term "Acme" is often used metaphorically to refer to the highest point or peak of something, representing excellence or the best in a particular field or category. It is not a specific definition but rather a concept or expression that signifies the pinnacle or zenith of achievement or quality. When people refer to something as the "Acme" of its kind, they mean it represents the absolute best or the highest standard within that category. Gracián's observation forces us to consider the evolving demands placed upon individuals striving for success and fulfillment. It beckons us to explore the interplay between knowledge, character, and adaptability in a world that challenges us in ways unimaginable to our predecessors.

The art of making one's way in the world has evolved into a sophisticated dance of skill and resilience. Success is no longer solely defined by wealth or social standing; it encompasses personal growth, emotional intelligence, and moral integrity. Modern life necessitates

balancing the demands of a fast-paced world with the values and principles that define our character.

Furthermore, interpersonal relationships in today's interconnected society have become intricate endeavors. Each person presents a unique set of needs, expectations, and complexities. Navigating these diverse relationships effectively requires empathy, understanding, and adaptability. Accordingly, pursuing wisdom and success is a multi-faceted journey that demands intellectual understanding, emotional intelligence, and ethical depth. It underscores the importance of being adaptable, discerning, and compassionate in a world where excellence is the benchmark. As we navigate the challenges and opportunities of our time, let us heed Gracián's wisdom and strive to reach our own Acme of wisdom and fulfillment.

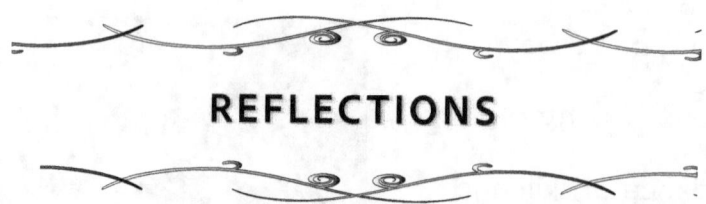

REFLECTIONS

- What are the specific challenges and demands of the contemporary world make it more challenging to become wise and knowledgeable? How have these challenges evolved?

- Explore the theme of adaptability in your life. How do you adapt to changing circumstances and challenges? Are there specific strategies or principles you follow to navigate the complexities of modern life?

- Consider that it takes more effort to deal with a single person today than with a whole person in the past. Reflect on your own experiences in dealing with individuals. How have interpersonal relationships changed in the modern world? What skills do you find essential in connecting with others?

- Think about individuals whom you consider wise or knowledgeable in today's world. What qualities or characteristics do they possess that make them stand out in your eyes? How can you learn from their experiences?

- Discuss your pursuit of excellence. In what areas of your life do you strive for the "Acme" or the highest level of achievement? How do you define and measure excellence in your own life?

- If you could go back in time and give advice to your younger self based on Gracián's quote, what would you say? How would this advice have impacted your journey?

- Consider your aspirations for wisdom, personal development, and dealing with others in the modern world. What steps can you take to continue growing and adapting in this ever-changing environment?

CRAFTING THE MODERN WISE SOUL REQUIRES SO MUCH MORE,

THAN WHAT WAS NECESSARY IN DAYS OF YORE.

FOR EACH STEP WE TAKE, EACH PATH WE FIND,

DEMANDS WISDOM OF A CERTAIN KIND

My Dear Friend,

In contemplating the aphorism, "Everything is at its acme, especially the art of making one's way in the world," one cannot help but discern its profound implications for our contemporary society. It speaks to the pinnacle of power and influences individuals strive to attain in our intricate world.

Indeed, in our age, the demands placed upon individuals to achieve wisdom and navigate the complexities of social hierarchy have never been more pressing. It is a world where astuteness and shrewdness reign supreme, where one must navigate the turbulent seas of politics and society with the precision of a seasoned sailor.

The "art of making one's way in the world" evokes the image of a master strategist, deftly maneuvering through the intricacies of human interaction to achieve their goals. In this regard, I am reminded of our discussions on the importance of diplomacy, negotiation, and persuasion in securing one's societal position.

Furthermore, consider the challenges posed by our dealings with individuals in this modern age. With the rise of individualism and the complexities of interpersonal relationships, we face a more intricate landscape than ever before. It is a world where adaptability and foresight are paramount, where one must navigate the subtle currents of human motivation with the skill of a seasoned navigator.

In conclusion, my dear friend, let us heed the wisdom of this aphorism and strive to master the art of making our way in the world. In doing so, we shall secure our success and shape the course of history itself.

Yours faithfully,

Niccolò Machiavelli

STRATEGIES

Strategic Networking: Build relationships with influential individuals to gain access to opportunities and insider knowledge.

Adaptability: Stay flexible and open-minded to navigate rapidly changing social dynamics and seize emerging opportunities.

Information Gathering: Acquire as much information as possible about people, organizations, and trends to make informed decisions and gain a competitive edge.

Manipulative Tactics: Utilize persuasion, manipulation, and cunning strategies to influence others and achieve desired outcomes.

Political Savvy: Understand the power dynamics within organizations and society and strategically position yourself to gain an advantage.

Risk Management: Assess potential risks and rewards of different courses of action and take calculated risks to advance your objectives.

Image Management: Cultivate a favorable public image and perception to enhance influence and credibility.

Exploiting Weaknesses: Identify and exploit the weaknesses of competitors or adversaries to gain a strategic advantage.

Resource Maximization: Efficiently allocate your resources, including time, money, and energy, to achieve the most significant impact.

Long-Term Vision: Develop and pursue long-term goals with patience and persistence while remaining adaptable to changing circumstances.

As we weave our plans,

May artful strategy guide hands.

Positioning ourselves skillfully to gain the might,

Necessary to dominate every fight.

2 - CHARACTER & INTELLECT

Character and Intellect are the two poles of our capacity; one without the other is halfway to happiness. Intellect sufficeth not; character is also needed. On the other hand, it is the fool's misfortune to fail to obtain the position, employment, neighborhood, and circle of friends that suit him.

At times, intellect is the cornerstone of success in the modern world. In a society driven by information, technology, and innovation, the value of intellectual prowess is undeniable. However, Gracián's assertion challenges us to consider that intellect alone is merely a fragment of the equation. Combining intellect and character forms the sturdy foundation upon which true happiness and fulfillment can be built.

Intellect, defined by cognitive abilities and knowledge, undoubtedly contributes to our capabilities and achievements. It equips us with the tools to analyze, strategize, and innovate. In pursuing a career or a goal, intellect often serves as the compass guiding us toward our objectives. However, as Gracián astutely observes, intellect suffices not. A person may possess a brilliant mind, yet without a solid character, they risk becoming a rudderless ship, navigating the seas of life aimlessly.

On the other hand, character encompasses a complex web of qualities and values that define an individual's moral and ethical compass. Integrity, honesty, empathy, resilience, and compassion are among the traits that comprise one's character. These qualities are the moral fiber that strengthens our interpersonal relationships, shapes our decisions, and ultimately defines our identity. Character enables us to navigate the complexities of human interaction and establish bonds of trust with others.

Gracián's wisdom is evident in the observation that one without the other is halfway to happiness. To illustrate this, consider a scenario where intellect reigns supreme but lacks character. Individuals with exceptional intellectual prowess may achieve professional success but are isolated or mistrusted by colleagues and friends. The absence of character can erode relationships and tarnish one's reputation, leaving a void in their pursuit of happiness.

Conversely, someone endowed with sterling character but lacking intellectual depth may struggle to unlock their full potential. They may possess empathy and kindness, yet without the intellectual capacity to channel these virtues effectively, their aspirations may remain unfulfilled. Character alone, while admirable, can only take an individual so far in the multifaceted landscape of life.

As Gracián describes it, the fool's misfortune lies in the inability to align one's character and intellect with their desired outcomes. It is a tragedy to fail to obtain the position, employment, neighborhood, or circle of friends that suits one's true self. This misalignment can result in a life marked by dissatisfaction, unfulfilled potential, and the perpetual sense of missing the mark.

In conclusion, character and intellect are not opposing forces but two interdependent pillars of our capacity. They are the dual keys to unlocking the door to happiness and fulfillment. The harmonious fusion of intellectual prowess and moral character is where the true magic happens in the intricate tapestry of human existence. In this balance, we discover the path to success, meaningful relationships, and a life well-lived.

REFLECTIONS

- Gracián suggests that character and intellect are necessary for happiness. Reflect on times in your life when you felt pleased. Can you attribute your happiness to a balance between your character and intellect? How did this balance manifest in your experiences?

- Explore how your character affects your relationships with others. How does your character shape your interactions with friends, family, and colleagues? Are there aspects of your character that you want to improve to enhance your relationships?

- Consider the role of intellect in your career or profession. How has your intellectual capacity influenced your job performance or career choices? Do you believe that character also plays a role in your professional success?

- Gracián mentions the fool's misfortune. Reflect on instances where you may have faced challenges or difficulties because of failing to obtain a position, job, neighborhood, or friends that truly suited you. What lessons have you learned from such experiences?

- What steps can you take to develop your character and intellect further? Are there specific areas of improvement you'd like to focus on? How do you envision these improvements benefiting your life?

- Consider the importance of making choices that align with your character and intellect. How can you ensure your decisions and actions align with your values and capabilities?

- Think about individuals you admire for their character and intellect. What qualities do they possess that you find inspiring? How can you incorporate some of these qualities into your own life?

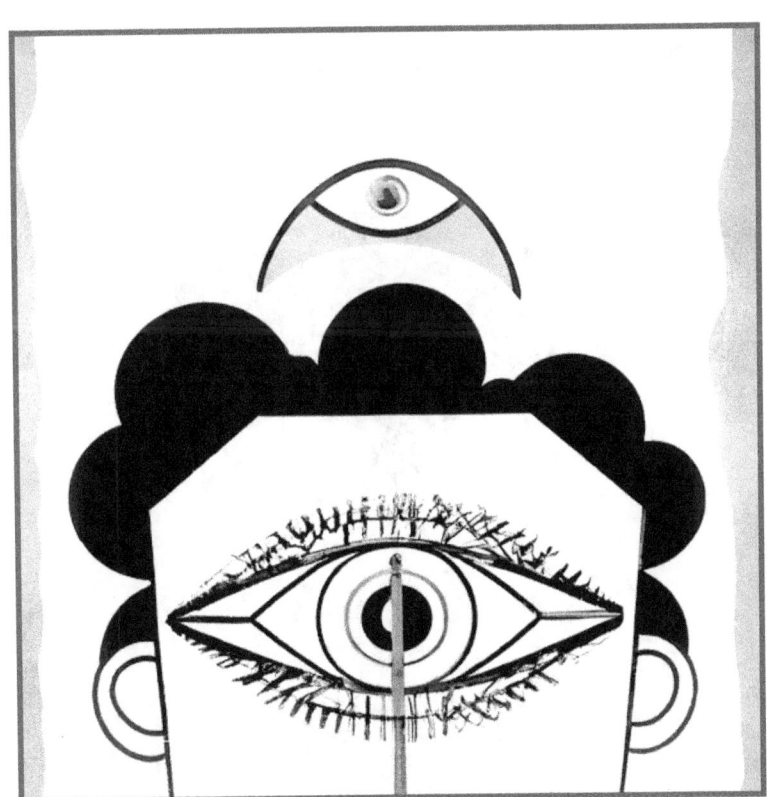

IN THE REALM OF LIFE'S VAST STAGE,

TWO PILLARS STAND, BOTH STRONG AND SAGE,

CHARACTER AND INTELLECT, THEY SAY,

ARE THE KEYS TO FIND OUR WAY.

My Dearest Reader,

In contemplating the counsel regarding character and intellect, we face a profound truth that resonates deeply with the essence of governance and personal advancement.

I'm curious: intellect, while undeniably valuable, is but one facet of the multifaceted gem that is power. It is the tool by which we analyze, strategize, and outmaneuver our adversaries. Yet, intellect alone is insufficient. My dear friend, the character is the bedrock upon which true power is built.

Think of character as the mortar that binds the bricks of intellect together. It is the embodiment of virtue, integrity, and strength of will. Without it, our intellectual prowess becomes hollow, devoid of the credibility and trust necessary to wield influence over others.

Consider the plight of the fool who fails to secure their desired position or social standing. This, my friend, is a cautionary tale of the consequences of neglecting either intellect or character. To achieve greatness, one must possess both in equal measure.

Therefore, let us heed this wisdom and strive to cultivate our minds and souls. Let us be shrewd in our intellect and unwavering in our character, for it is through this harmonious union that we shall ascend to the pinnacle of power and influence.

Yours in contemplation and strategy,

Niccolò Machiavelli

STRATEGIES

Cultivate a balance between intellect and character: While intellect may grant you knowledge and insight, character will ultimately determine your credibility and influence.

Prioritize self-awareness and personal development: Continuously assess and improve your intellectual capabilities and moral character to ensure they align with your goals and aspirations.

Build a reputation of integrity and reliability: Act with honesty, integrity, and consistency in all your dealings to earn the trust and respect of others, thereby enhancing your ability to influence and lead.

Develop strategic alliances and networks: Surround yourself with individuals with complementary strengths and virtues, leveraging their intellect and character to augment your own.

Exercise discernment in decision-making: Consider the intellectual implications of your choices and the ethical and moral consequences, ensuring that your actions reflect sound judgment and virtuous character.

Embrace humility and self-reflection: Remain open to feedback and criticism, acknowledging your limitations and striving for continual growth and improvement in intellect and character.

Cultivate empathy and emotional intelligence: Understand the perspectives and motivations of others and use this insight to forge deeper connections and inspire loyalty, demonstrating intellectual understanding and emotional maturity.

Lead by example: Model the values and behaviors you wish to instill in others, embodying the virtues of both intellect and character in your words and actions.

Never underestimate the power of perseverance: Recognize that success is often the result of sustained effort and resilience in the face of adversity, demonstrating both intellectual tenacity and moral courage.

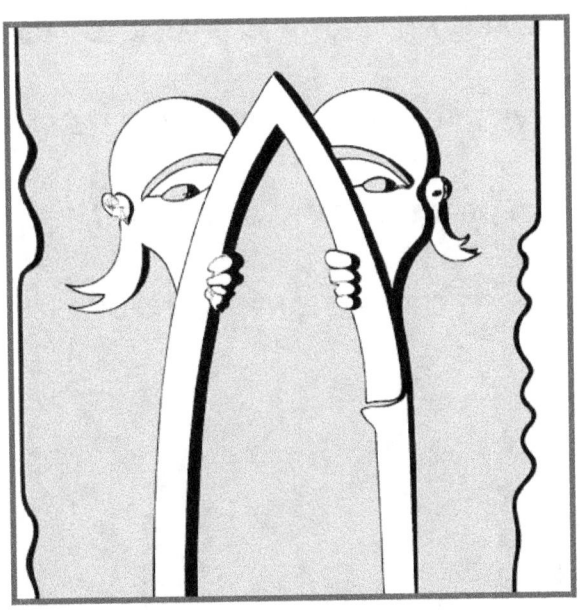

LEVERAGE INTELLECT AND CHARACTER ALIKE,

AND WATCH YOUR INFLUENCE TAKE ITS SPIKE.

FOR INTEGRITY AND RELIABILITY,

ARE THE CORNERSTONES OF CREDIBILITY.

Keep Matters for a Time in Suspense | Admiration at their novelty heightens the value of your achievements; playing with the cards on the table is both useless and tasteless. If you do not declare yourself immediately, you arouse expectation, especially when the importance of your position makes you the object of general attention. Mix a little mystery with everything, and the very mystery arouses veneration. And when you explain, be not too explicit, just as you do not expose your innermost thoughts in ordinary intercourse. Cautious silence is the holy of holies of worldly wisdom. A resolution declared is never highly thought of; it only leaves room for criticism. And if it happens to fail, you are doubly unfortunate. Besides, you imitate the Divine way when you cause men to wonder and watch.

Baltasar Gracián's counsel, "Keep Matters for a Time in Suspense," provides profound insights into strategic ambiguity and calculated restraint. It is a strategy that not only enhances the value of our endeavors but also cultivates an aura of intrigue and reverence, elevating us to a position of distinction in the eyes of others.

One of the most compelling reasons for keeping matters in suspense is the heightened admiration it engenders for our achievements. In a world saturated with information and constant disclosure, novelty has become a rare and precious commodity. When we withhold immediate declaration, we create a sense of anticipation, allowing others to marvel at the unveiling of our accomplishments. This anticipation magnifies the perceived value of our endeavors, transforming them into objects of fascination and admiration.

Furthermore, Gracián's counsel underscores that transparency can often be bland and unimpressive. Playing with "cards on the table," so to speak, diminishes the intrigue and allure that shrouds our actions and decisions. By contrast, our actions' deliberate dose of mystery captivates and engages our audience, drawing them into a narrative of curiosity and fascination.

In the realm of public perception and attention, timing is of paramount importance. Gracián's wisdom becomes particularly relevant when one occupies a position of significance and attention. A premature declaration of one's intentions or actions can trigger heightened expectations, often leading to scrutiny and critique. By keeping matters in suspense, we retain the element of surprise and maintain a degree of control over the narrative that unfolds.

The very essence of mystery is a powerful force. It can arouse veneration, an acknowledgment that what is concealed may hold profound significance. By preserving an aura of enigma around our actions and decisions, we invite others to marvel at our wisdom and strategic prowess. In this space of wonder, admiration, and respect, find fertile ground to flourish.

Moreover, Gracián's counsel encourages us to exercise discretion when explaining ourselves. Just as we do not reveal our innermost thoughts in ordinary conversation, we should exercise caution in disclosing the full extent of our intentions and strategies. Cautious silence, as  Gracián terms it, is the holy of holies of worldly wisdom. It allows us to control the narrative, preventing premature judgment and criticism.

A resolution declared prematurely is often met with skepticism and leaves little room for imagination. It is akin to laying all our cards on the table, leaving us vulnerable to critique and the risk of failure. Gracián's wisdom reminds us that when we retain an element of mystery, we not only preserve the intrigue but also maintain the flexibility to adapt our course of action as circumstances evolve.

In essence, keeping matters in suspense is a powerful tool that allows us to navigate the complexities of human interaction and achievement with finesse and grace. It is a strategy that enhances the value of our endeavors, invites admiration, and preserves our agency in the face of scrutiny. By imitating the Divine way of causing wonder and watchfulness, we elevate ourselves to a position of distinction and mastery in worldly wisdom.

REFLECTIONS

- Have you ever experienced a situation where you felt like you were "playing cards on the table," being too open or explicit about your intentions? How did it impact the outcome? Reflect on what you could have done differently to introduce an element of mystery.

- Consider when you intentionally delayed declaring your intentions or actions. How did it affect the expectations of others, especially in situations where you held an important position or were in the spotlight? Reflect on the power of expectation in various aspects of life.

- Explore integrating a sense of mystery into your daily life or projects. Are there situations where you can benefit from keeping specific details concealed or revealing them gradually to spark curiosity and admiration?

- Reflect on your communication style. Are there instances where you tend to be overly explicit or reveal too much too soon? How might you practice being less explicit in your interactions, as Gracián suggests, without compromising clarity?

- Consider a situation where you openly declared a resolution or intention and faced criticism or did not go as planned. How might keeping matters in suspense have influenced the outcome? Reflect on lessons learned from these experiences.

- Consider how embracing the wisdom of keeping matters in suspense can contribute to your personal growth and mastery of worldly wisdom. How can you integrate these principles into your ongoing journey of self-improvement?

EXPLAIN LITTLE, LEST THE MAGIC WANE,

LEAVE ROOM FOR WONDER, LET MYSTERY REIGN.

FOR CAUTIOUS SILENCE IS THE WISDOM'S CREED,

WITHIN IT LIES THE POWER WE ALL NEED.

My Dear Friend,

In the art of statecraft, a principle of paramount importance exists—a principle that, if mastered, can secure one's position of power and influence amidst the ebb and flow of political tides. This principle is none other than the strategic use of suspense—a calculated withholding of information and resolution designed to evoke admiration and respect from those around you.

As you navigate the intricate terrain of political maneuvering, I urge you to heed the wisdom of keeping matters in suspense for a time. Embrace the allure of novelty and mystery, for they can elevate the perception of your achievements and enhance your standing in the eyes of others. By withholding immediate declarations and explanations, you can cultivate an air of anticipation and curiosity, drawing others into your orbit with the irresistible allure of the unknown.

Remember, my friend, that caution is the cornerstone of worldly wisdom. Just as one does not reveal their innermost thoughts in casual conversation, so must you exercise discretion in matters of statecraft. Let your words be measured, your intentions veiled, and your actions imbued with mystery. In doing so, you will command the respect and admiration of those around you, for you will emulate the divine in your ability to inspire wonder and awe.

In pursuing power and influence, there is no more excellent asset than the strategic use of suspense. Embrace this principle, my friend, and wield it skillfully and precisely. For in the art of statecraft, as in all things, it is the master of suspense who reigns supreme.

Yours faithfully,

Niccolò Machiavelli

STRATEGIES

Embrace novelty: Introduce new ideas, initiatives, or projects to captivate attention and evoke admiration for your achievements.

Maintain ambiguity: Avoid revealing all your intentions or plans immediately, keeping others in suspense and heightening their curiosity.

Use mystery to your advantage: Infuse an element of mystery into your actions and communications to arouse awe and respect from those around you.

Exercise discretion in explanations: When providing explanations or justifications, refrain from being overly explicit, leaving room for interpretation, and maintaining an air of intrigue.

Value cautious silence: Recognize the power of silence as a strategic tool, using it to convey wisdom, prudence, and control over one's words and actions.

Avoid premature declarations: Refrain from hastily declaring your resolutions or plans, as premature announcements can invite criticism and diminish their perceived value.

Imitate the divine: Emulate the enigmatic nature of the divine by causing others to wonder and watch your every move, enhancing your aura of authority and influence.

Cultivate an aura of anticipation: Create anticipation and expectation around your actions and decisions by strategically delaying declarations or explanations.

Capitalize on the element of surprise: Employ unexpected or unconventional tactics to catch others off guard and assert your dominance in various situations.

Maintain an air of mystery: Keep certain aspects of your persona or agenda hidden from public view, allowing others to speculate and attribute greater significance to your actions.

EMULATING THE DIVINE, WE CAST OUR SPELL,

STRATEGICALLY PLOTTING AS WE EXCEL.

MAINTAINING MYSTERY IS KEY TO OUR ART,

OBSCURE WHATEVER ISN'T VITAL TO OUR PART.

4 - KNOWLEDGE AND COURAGE

Knowledge and Courage are the elements of Greatness. They give immortality because they are immortal. Each is as much as he knows, and the wise can do anything. A man without knowledge, a world without light. Wisdom and strength, eyes and hands. Knowledge without courage is sterile.

True greatness is not merely about acquiring information or exhibiting bravery but the harmonious fusion of both attributes. Knowledge, the foundation upon which wisdom is built, is a wellspring of inexhaustible power. It grants individuals the ability to discern, innovate, and navigate the complexities of life. The pursuit of knowledge is a lifelong endeavor, and it serves as a constant source of growth and self-improvement. Those who aspire to greatness recognize that knowledge is not a finite resource but an eternal well of inspiration that fuels their aspirations.

Courage, often synonymous with bravery, is equally instrumental in pursuing greatness. It empowers individuals to overcome fear, adversity, and uncertainty. Courage is not the absence of fear but the willingness to act in the face of it. It is the audacity to step into the unknown and embrace challenges head-on. It is the force that propels individuals toward their goals and encourages them to push boundaries.

Gracián's assertion that knowledge and courage give immortality speaks to the enduring impact that individuals can have when they possess these qualities. Greatness is not fleeting; it endures through the ages because it is based on attributes that transcend time and circumstance. Those who acquire knowledge and cultivate courage leave an indelible mark on the world, shaping history.

The notion that "Each is as much as he knows" reinforces the idea that knowledge is the measure of an individual's potential. The more one knows, the greater their capacity to effect change and contribute to society. Knowledge is a well-rounded tool that enhances problem-solving, decision-making, and creative thinking. It is the currency of progress and innovation.

Wisdom and strength, represented by knowledge and courage, are indispensable companions on the path to greatness. Wisdom enables individuals to apply their knowledge judiciously, fostering discernment and ethical decision-making. Strength, in the form of courage, provides the fortitude to act on that wisdom, even in the face of formidable challenges.

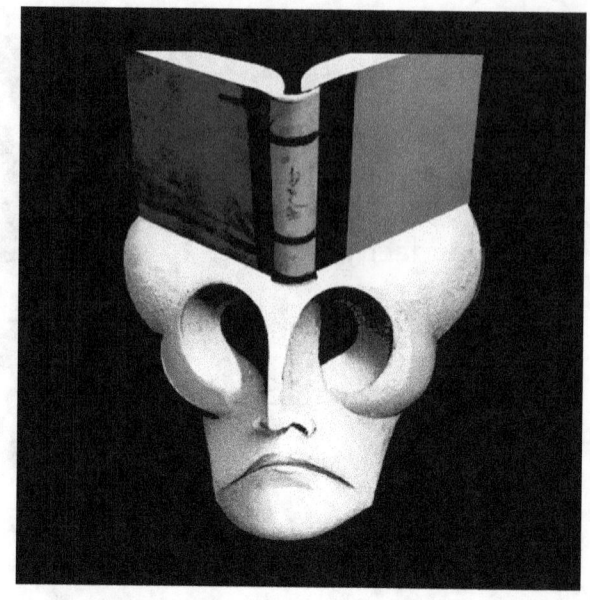

However, knowledge without courage remains sterile, a mere accumulation of facts without the impetus for action. It is courage that transforms knowledge into meaningful impact. Courage is the spark that ignites the engine of change, propelling individuals to put their knowledge to practical use.

Developing knowledge and courage requires intention and effort. To cultivate knowledge, one must be committed to lifelong learning. This includes reading, seeking diverse perspectives, and engaging in meaningful experiences that broaden one's horizons. Knowledge is nurtured through curiosity, inquiry, and a thirst for understanding.

Courage, on the other hand, demands self-awareness and self-belief. It requires individuals to confront their fears and take calculated risks. Developing courage is a gradual process that involves stepping outside one's comfort zone and embracing discomfort as a catalyst for growth.

In conclusion, the pursuit of greatness is anchored in the synthesis of knowledge and courage. These immortal elements elevate individuals to heights of enduring influence and impact. Knowledge equips us with the tools of wisdom, while courage empowers us to act upon that wisdom. To attain greatness is to embark on a lifelong journey of learning, growth, and audacious action. Individuals can leave a lasting legacy through the fusion of knowledge and courage, illuminating the world for generations to come.

REFLECTIONS

- Reflect on a time when your knowledge or courage was tested. How did you respond, and what did you learn from the experience?

- Consider the areas of your life where you feel most knowledgeable. How has this knowledge contributed to your sense of confidence and fulfillment?

- Think about a situation where you needed courage but lacked the necessary knowledge. How did you navigate this challenge, and what could you do differently in the future?

- Explore the concept of immortality through knowledge and courage. What does it mean to you to leave a lasting legacy through your actions and decisions?

- Contemplate the relationship between wisdom and strength in your life. How do these qualities complement each other, and how can you cultivate both to achieve greatness?

- Reflect on the idea that knowledge without courage is sterile. Are there areas of your life where you possess knowledge but struggle to take action? What steps can you take to overcome this barrier?

- Consider the role of light as a metaphor for knowledge. How does acquiring knowledge illuminate your path and guide your decisions?

- Reflect on the importance of balance between knowledge and courage. How can you ensure you continue cultivating both qualities in your life?

- Explore how your knowledge and courage empower you to impact the world around you positively.

- Reflect on a person you admire who exemplifies the qualities of knowledge and courage. What lessons can you learn from their example, and how can you apply them to your own life?

KNOWLEDGE GRANTS US POWER AND UNLOCKS DOORS,

ENABLING FEATS NEVER DREAMT BEFORE.

BUT COURAGE, TOO, IS A CRUCIAL PART,

IT'S THE FIRE IN OUR SOULS THAT IGNITES OUR HEART.

———

My Dearest Friend,

In our pursuit of greatness and power, let us remember the invaluable importance of knowledge and courage. These two elements are the very essence of immortality, for they endure beyond the constraints of time and mortality.

Knowledge, my friend, is the cornerstone of greatness. It grants us the understanding and insight to navigate the complexities of our world. With knowledge, we can decipher human nature's intricacies, anticipate our adversaries' moves, and craft strategies that will lead us to victory. Without knowledge, we are but blind wanderers in a world of chaos and uncertainty, unable to discern truth from falsehood or to grasp the opportunities that lie before us.

Yet, knowledge alone is not enough. It must be coupled with courage—the unwavering resolve to act in adversity. Courage drives effective leadership, enabling us to make bold decisions and assert our will upon the world. With courage, we can overcome the obstacles that stand in our path, confront our enemies with steely determination, and seize the opportunities that others dare not pursue. Without courage, knowledge remains dormant and ineffectual, a mere shadow of its true potential.

My friend, knowledge, and courage together form the bedrock of greatness. They empower us to leave a lasting legacy, shape history, and attain a form of immortality that transcends the limitations of our mortal existence. Therefore, let us cultivate these virtues diligently, for in them lies the key to our success and enduring influence upon the world.

Yours faithfully,

Niccolò Machiavelli

STRATEGIES

Continuously seek knowledge: Machiavelli would advise constantly expanding one's understanding of the world through reading, studying, and learning from various sources.

Develop strategic thinking: Machiavelli would suggest honing the ability to analyze situations critically and anticipate potential outcomes, allowing one to make informed decisions.

Embrace calculated risks: Machiavelli would advocate for having the courage to take bold actions when necessary, even if they involve risks, as long as they are calculated and based on a thorough understanding of the situation.

Cultivate resilience: Machiavelli stresses the importance of courage in facing adversity and setbacks with resilience, refusing to be deterred by obstacles or failures.

Seize opportunities: Machiavelli would advise recognizing and seizing opportunities for advancement or success, leveraging one's knowledge and courage to capitalize on favorable circumstances.

Lead by example: Machiavelli would encourage demonstrating wisdom and strength in leadership, inspiring others through actions and decisions.

Build alliances: Machiavelli would suggest forging strategic alliances with individuals or groups with complementary knowledge and resources, enhancing one's capabilities and influence.

Maintain a strong reputation: Machiavelli would recommend cultivating a reputation for wisdom, courage, and integrity, as it enhances one's credibility and influence in both personal and professional spheres.

FORTUNE FAVORS THE BRAVE AND THE BOLD,

WHO SEIZE OPPORTUNITIES, AS THEY UNFOLD.

WITH KNOWLEDGE AS OUR CORNERSTONE,

WE EMBRACE THE COURAGE TO FACE THE UNKNOWN.

5 - CREATE A FEELING OF DEPENDENCE

Not he that adorns, but he that adores makes a divinity. The wise man would rather see men needing him than thanking him. To keep them on the threshold of hope is diplomatic, to trust their gratitude boorish; hope has a good memory, gratitude a bad one. More is to be got from dependence than from courtesy. He that has satisfied his thirst turns his back on the well, and the orange, once sucked, falls from the golden platter into the waste basket. When dependence disappears, good behavior goes with it, as well as respect. Let it be one of the chief lessons of experience to keep hope alive without entirely satisfying it by preserving it to make oneself always needed, even by a patron on the throne. But let not silence be carried to excess lest you go wrong, nor let another's failing grow incurable for your advantage.

These words suggest genuine admiration and respect, rather than superficial adornment, elevate individuals to a divine status. The wise man values being needed over receiving thanks, recognizing that dependency fosters a more profound connection than mere courtesy.

Keeping others on the threshold of hope is deemed diplomatic, as it maintains their reliance without breeding complacency. Trusting solely in gratitude is seen as coarse, as hope possesses a lasting memory while gratitude often fades.

Rather than courtesy, dependence yields more significant benefits, fostering loyalty and respect. However, once satisfaction is achieved, complacency sets in, and both good behavior and respect wane.

Experience teaches the importance of preserving hope without entirely satisfying it. Maintaining a sense of need ensures continued relevance and importance, even in the most influential circles.

Silence should be balanced; excessive silence may lead to misunderstandings or missed opportunities. Similarly, exploiting another's failing for personal gain

is cautioned against, as it risks damaging relationships and integrity.

These insights remind us of the delicate balance between fostering reliance and preserving autonomy, hope's enduring power, and integrity's importance in all dealings with others.

REFLECTIONS

- Reflect on instances in your life where you've experienced the difference between being needed versus being thanked. How did it feel to be relied upon versus appreciated?

- Consider when you've relied on someone else for support or guidance. How did their ability to maintain hope without fully satisfying your needs impact your perception of them?

- Explore the concept of dependence versus courtesy in your interactions with others. Have you found that cultivating dependence leads to more favorable outcomes than simply being courteous?

- Think about a situation where you or someone else has satisfied a desire only for it to lead to complacency and a loss of respect. How could this have been avoided or mitigated?

- Reflect on a time when you've witnessed someone's behavior change due to a shift in their dependence on others. How did this impact their actions and relationships?

- Consider the balance between preserving hope and avoiding excess silence. Have you ever found yourself in a situation where silence was detrimental to your goals or relationships?

- Explore the ethical implications of exploiting another's failing for personal advantage. Have you ever witnessed or experienced this in your own life? How did it affect your perception of the individual involved?

- Reflect on the lessons you've learned from experiences where you've either maintained hope without entirely satisfying it or witnessed others do so. How have these lessons shaped your approach to relationships and power dynamics?

THE WISE MAN KNOWS, IT'S BETTER TO BE,

NEEDED IN WANT THAN THANKED WITH GLEE.

FOR HOPE IS A FUEL THAT BURNS SO BRIGHT,

WHILE GRATITUDE FADES IN THE DEAD OF NIGHT.

———

My Dearest Friend,

In the art of governance and influence, I have long believed that true power lies not in superficial adornments or empty praise but in the genuine adoration and dependence of those around us. Your recent inquiries have prompted me to share some Machiavellian wisdom.

Remember, it is far more advantageous to be needed than merely thanked. Dependence fosters a stronger bond and ensures continued loyalty, while gratitude often fades quickly. As such, it is imperative to cultivate a sense of dependency among those you seek to influence.

Maintaining a delicate balance between hope and satisfaction is also crucial. While offering hope and keeping individuals on the expectation threshold is diplomatically shrewd, relying solely on gratitude is seen as ineffective. The wise leader can leverage dependence to extract more significant benefits and maintain control over others.

Beware of complacency and the danger of allowing dependence to wane. Once an individual's thirst is satisfied, they are prone to turn away from the source of their satisfaction, leading to a loss of influence and respect. Therefore, even if it means withholding complete satisfaction, perpetuating dependence and hope is critical to maintaining power.

However, one must also exercise caution against excessive silence or allowing others' failures to become incurable solely for personal advantage. While it is essential to maintain dependence and hope, ethical boundaries must be respected to avoid alienating allies or causing irreparable harm.

In conclusion, my friend, remember that true greatness lies in the adoration and dependence of those around us. We can ensure our continued influence and power by mastering the art of dependency and carefully balancing hope and satisfaction.

Yours faithfully,

Niccolò Machiavelli

STRATEGIES

Maintain hope: Keep individuals on the threshold of hope by offering glimpses of potential satisfaction without fully satisfying their desires. Hopeful individuals are more likely to remain loyal and cooperative.

Avoid excessive gratitude: Trusting solely in the gratitude of others is seen as coarse and ineffective. Instead, focus on cultivating dependence, as hope has a longer-lasting impact than gratitude.

Preserve and exploit dependency: Ensure that individuals continue to require your assistance and guidance, as this perpetuates your influence and power.

Balance satisfaction: Be wary of satisfying individuals' desires too quickly, which may lead to a loss of respect and dependency. Instead, maintain a delicate balance between satisfying their needs and keeping them longing for more.

Beware of silence: While maintaining an air of mystery can be advantageous, excessive silence can lead to misunderstandings or missed opportunities. Ensure that your intentions and desires are communicated effectively to avoid confusion.

Capitalize on others' failings: Use the failings of others to reinforce your position of power, but be careful not to allow these failings to become incurable for your benefit.

Cultivate a sense of need: Position yourself as indispensable to those in positions of power, ensuring that they always rely on your expertise and support.

Exercise caution: While Machiavellian strategies can effectively gain and maintain power, it is essential to exercise caution and avoid overstepping ethical boundaries. Balancing ambition with prudence is critical to long-term success.

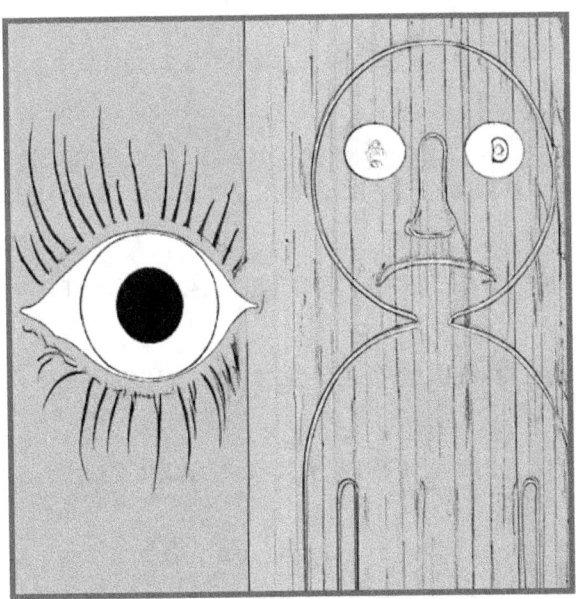

FOR HOPE REMEMBERS, WHILE GRATITUDE FORGETS,

DEPENDENCY YIELDS FAR MORE, THAN COURTESY BEGETS.

SO PRESERVE AND EXPLOIT THE NEED FOR YOU.

VIA DEPENDENCY, YOUR POWER RENEWS.

6 - A MAN AT HIS HIGHEST POINT

A Man at His Highest Point | We are not born perfect: every day, we develop our personality and calling till we reach the highest point of our completed being, to the whole round of our accomplishments, of our excellences. This is known by the purity of our taste, the clearness of our thought, the maturity of our judgment, and the firmness of our will. Some never arrive at being complete; somewhat is always lacking; others ripen late. The complete man, wise in speech, prudent in act, is admitted to the familiar intimacy of discreet persons and is even sought for by them.

Perfection isn't a static state but a continuous process of growth and refinement. Individuals embark on personal and professional evolution from birth, honing their character and talents.

The concept of reaching one's highest point suggests achieving a state of completeness in various aspects of life. This includes external accomplishments and inner qualities such as purity of taste, clarity of thought, maturity of judgment, and firmness of will. These traits reflect a deep understanding of oneself and the world, guiding actions and decisions with wisdom and prudence.

However, pursuing completeness is not universal; some individuals never attain it, while others mature later in life. This highlights the uniqueness of each person's journey and the diverse paths to fulfillment.

A "complete" person embodies these qualities fully, becoming a beacon of insight and integrity. Such individuals are admired and sought after for their wisdom and discretion. They navigate social interactions with grace and wisdom, earning the trust and respect of those around them.

True fulfillment lies not in reaching a destination but in the journey itself, marked by continual growth, self-awareness, and the cultivation of noble qualities.

REFLECTIONS

- Reflect on a recent experience where you felt a sense of personal growth or development. How did this experience contribute to your journey towards becoming your highest self?

- Consider the qualities of "purity of taste," "clearness of thought," "maturity of judgment," and "firmness of will." Which of these qualities do you feel you possess most strongly? Which ones do you aspire to develop further, and why?

- Explore a time when you faced a challenging decision. How did you navigate this situation, and what factors influenced your judgment? Reflect on whether your actions aligned with the qualities of a "complete man" described in the passage.

- Think about individuals in your life whom you consider to embody the characteristics of a "complete man." What specific traits or behaviors do they exhibit that you admire? How can you incorporate some of these qualities into your own life?

- Consider the idea that "some never arrive at being complete; somewhat is always lacking." Reflect on areas of your life where you feel incomplete or where there is room for growth. What steps can you take to address these areas and move closer to your highest potential?

- Write about a time when you felt a deep sense of intimacy or connection with someone you consider discreet and wise. What qualities did this person possess that drew you to them? How did this relationship contribute to your personal growth and development?

- Imagine yourself as the "complete man" described in the passage. What would your life look like? How would you interact with others, make decisions, and pursue your goals? Use this vision to inspire and guide your actions moving forward.

Our taste refined, our thoughts so clear,

Our judgment mature, our will sincere.

We seek completeness, strive for grace,

With every action, we secure our place.

———

My Dear Friend,

In contemplating reaching one's highest point, I am reminded of the profound journey of self-discovery and development we undertake throughout our lives. It is not a journey marked by innate perfection but rather a continual process of growth and refinement, wherein every day presents an opportunity for advancement in our character and our pursuits.

As we navigate this journey, we strive towards the culmination of our being, a state characterized by the purity of our taste, the clarity of our thought, the maturity of our judgment, and the firmness of our will. When fully realized, these qualities reflect the completeness of our accomplishments and herald our ascent to the highest point of our existence.

Yet, my friend, it is essential to recognize that not all individuals reach this state of completeness. Some may falter along the way, perpetually falling short of their potential, while others may mature later in life, their development taking a more gradual and winding path.

Nevertheless, those who achieve completeness are distinguished by their wisdom in speech and prudence in action. They are held in high esteem by those who value discretion and are sought after for their insight and discernment. This familiarity and intimacy with discreet individuals makes their completeness most keenly felt and acknowledged.

In conclusion, my friend, let us embrace the journey toward completeness with courage and determination, knowing that it is through continuous self-reflection and growth that we inch ever closer to our highest point. May we embody wisdom and prudence in all our endeavors, thus leaving a lasting legacy of greatness for generations to come.

Yours sincerely,

Niccolò Machiavelli

STRATEGIES

Continual self-improvement: Embrace the idea that perfection is not innate but a continual development process. Dedicate yourself to daily growth in your personality and pursuits.

Cultivate purity of taste: Develop a discerning palate and refine your aesthetic sensibilities. Seek out experiences that broaden your cultural and intellectual horizons, allowing you to develop a refined sense of taste.

Cultivate clear thinking: Practice critical thinking and logical reasoning to cultivate clarity of thought. Engage in intellectual pursuits that challenge your mind and broaden your perspective.

Develop mature judgment: Make decisions based on careful consideration and sound reasoning. Reflect on past experiences to learn from your mistakes and refine your judgment.

Strengthen your willpower: Cultivate resilience and determination to overcome obstacles and achieve your goals. Develop a solid self-discipline to stay focused and committed to your objectives.

Surround yourself with discretion: Earn the trust and respect of discreet individuals by demonstrating wisdom in speech and prudence in action. Cultivate relationships with those who value discretion and seek their company.

Strive for completeness: Aim to reach your highest point by embodying wisdom, prudence, and integrity in all aspects of your life. Work towards becoming a well-rounded individual with a strong character and moral compass.

Remain humble: Despite your achievements, maintain humility and a willingness to learn from others. Recognize that true greatness lies not in self-aggrandizement but in the continuous pursuit of excellence.

IF YOU SEEK COMPLETENESS, IN MIND AND IN SOUL,

EMBODY WISDOM, PRUDENCE, AND CONTROL.

FOR IN THE PURSUIT OF EXCELLENCE, WE FIND,

THE ESSENCE OF GREATNESS IN OUR HEART AND MIND.

7 - AVOID VICTORIES OVER SUPERIORS

All victories breed hate, and that over your superior is foolish or fatal. Superiority is always detested, à fortiori* superiority over superiority. Caution can gloss over common advantages; for example, careless attire may cloak good looks. Some will grant you precedence in good luck or a good temper, but none in a good sense, least of all a prince; for good sense is a royal prerogative, any claim to that is a case of lèse majesté (i.e., treason). They are princes and wish to be so in that most princely qualities. They will allow a man to help them but not to surpass them and will have any advice tendered to them appear like a recollection of something they have forgotten rather than as a guide to something they cannot find. The stars teach us this finesse with happy tact; though they are his children and brilliant like him, they never rival the brilliancy of the sun.

* "À fortiori" is a Latin term that translates to "with stronger reason" or "all the more so" in English.

With these words, Baltasar Gracián delves into the intricate dynamics of power and superiority. It suggests that triumphing over one's superior breeds hatred, which can lead to dire consequences. Being perceived as superior is detested, especially by those who hold superiority themselves.

Gracián emphasizes the importance of caution in managing advantages. For instance, one's good looks may be overshadowed by careless attire. Even though some may concede precedence in luck or temperament, none will yield in a good sense, especially superiors who consider it a royal prerogative.

Superiors, Gracián notes, are particularly sensitive to challenges to their intellect. They may accept assistance but resist being surpassed. Their ego demands that guidance be presented as a gentle reminder, not a directive.

Gracián uses the analogy of stars and the sun to illustrate this finesse. Stars, though brilliant, never rival the radiance of the sun. Similarly, those in positions of power may accept assistance but guard against any perceived challenge to their authority.

REFLECTIONS

- Reflect on a time when you achieved a victory or success. How did others react to your achievement? Did you encounter any feelings of hatred or jealousy from those around you?

- Consider a situation where you had to interact with someone in a position of authority or superiority. How did you navigate this interaction? Did you find balancing respect for their position with your capabilities and opinions challenging?

- Explore the concept of superiority and how it is perceived in society. Do you believe that superiority is always detested, as Gracián suggests? How do you feel about those perceived as superior to others?

- Reflect on instances where caution helped you navigate advantages or disadvantages in your life. How did you use caution to mitigate potential challenges or pitfalls?

- Think about the qualities that are valued in different social contexts. Are certain traits, like good sense or intelligence, universally admired? How do people react to those who possess these qualities?

- Consider the analogy of stars and the sun as used by Gracián. How does this analogy apply to interpersonal relationships and dynamics of power? Reflect on times when you observed this finesse in action.

- Reflect on your aspirations for success and achievement. How do you balance ambition with humility? How do you navigate relationships with those who may be more successful or accomplished than you?

Remember as your victories won,

That hate and envy arise when one's undone.

Thus, to triumph over one's superior,

Can lead to a position more inferior.

———

My Dearest Friend,

In contemplating Baltasar Gracián's aphorism, "All victories breed hate, and that over your superior is foolish or fatal," I am reminded of the delicate dance one must perform in matters of superiority. I approach the subject with great caution and astuteness, for the consequences of a misstep can be dire indeed.

As you know, in politics and power, the display of superiority, particularly over one's superiors, can provoke resentment and hostility. Such resentment, left unchecked, can decay into a dangerous force that threatens to undermine one's position and authority. Therefore, we must tread lightly in matters of superiority lest we incur the wrath of those we seek to surpass.

Gracián's wisdom teaches us the importance of finesse and subtlety in navigating situations where we find ourselves in a position of superiority. Rather than flaunting our advantages overtly, we must employ tact and discretion, concealing our superiority in a manner that does not arouse envy or resentment in others.

Moreover, we must be mindful of the mindset of those in positions of power, particularly princes and rulers. They are naturally suspicious of those who seek to surpass them, especially in matters of intellect or wisdom, which they perceive as their exclusive domain. Therefore, any attempt to offer counsel or guidance to such individuals must be made with the utmost care, ensuring that it does not challenge their authority or sense of superiority.

In essence, my friend Gracián's aphorism serves as a poignant reminder of the complexities inherent in matters of superiority. We hope to maintain our position and influence in the tumultuous world of politics and power through careful navigation and strategic finesse.

Yours faithfully,

Niccolò Machiavelli

STRATEGIES

Employ Discretion: Avoid openly flaunting superiority, especially over superiors, to prevent resentment and hostility.

Exercise Tact: Use finesse and subtlety to conceal superiority, ensuring it does not provoke envy or resentment in others.

Be Mindful of Authority Figures: Understand the mindset of those in power, particularly princes and rulers, who may view challenges to their superiority as threats to their authority.

Offer Counsel Carefully: When providing advice or guidance to authority figures, do so cautiously, ensuring it does not challenge their sense of superiority or authority.

Conceal Brilliance: If possessing superior qualities or intellect, avoid overt displays that may provoke jealousy or resentment among peers or superiors.

Maintain a Modest Demeanor: Present oneself modestly, downplaying one's advantages or superior qualities to avoid arousing envy or resentment.

Strive for Subtlety: Employ subtle tactics to showcase superiority without overtly challenging the authority or superiority of others.

Be Aware of Jealousy: Recognize that victories or displays of superiority may breed jealousy or resentment, particularly among peers or superiors.

Exercise Caution in Competition: Approach competition and conflicts with superiors carefully, avoiding unnecessary displays of superiority that may provoke hostility.

In the game of life, discretion's key,

So navigate with subtlety.

With finesse and skill, you must carefully proceed

To exercise tact in every deed,

8 - TO BE WITHOUT PASSIONS

To be without passions 'tis a privilege of the highest order of mind. Their very eminence redeems them from being affected by transient and low impulses. There is no higher rule than that over oneself, over one's impulses: there is the triumph of free will. While passion rules the character, no aiming at the high office; the less, the higher, it is the only refined way of avoiding scandals; nay, 'tis the shortest way back to a good reputation.

motional detachment and self-mastery represent the pinnacle of human achievement. Those with such a state of mind are elevated above the influence of transient and base impulses. Their eminence shields them from being swayed by momentary desires or emotions.

Gracián emphasizes the importance of self-rule and mastery over one's impulses as the ultimate expression of autonomy and free will. This triumph over oneself signifies a profound victory, enabling individuals to navigate life with clarity and purpose, liberated from the tyranny of passion.

Furthermore, Gracián argues that allowing passions to rule one's character inhibits pursuing noble goals and exceptionally high office. Passion, he contends, clouds judgment and leads to scandal, tarnishing one's reputation. Therefore, those aspiring to leadership must strive for emotional equilibrium and detachment.

Gracián advocates for a refined and disciplined approach to life characterized by emotional detachment and self-control. Individuals can uphold their dignity, integrity, and reputation by transcending transient impulses and reigning over their passions.

Ultimately, to be without passions is not a state of apathy but rather a state of serenity and inner peace. It is maintaining composure and clarity of thought in the face of adversity. Individuals can navigate life's challenges with grace and resilience by cultivating emotional detachment, restoring a good reputation, and attaining true fulfillment.

REFLECTIONS

- Reflect on a time when you felt deeply passionate about something. How did these passions influence your thoughts, actions, and decisions? Were there any consequences, positive or negative, as a result of these passions?

- Consider the concept of emotional detachment and self-mastery. Do you believe that being without passions is a privilege of the highest order of mind, as suggested by Gracián? Why or why not?

- Explore instances where you've experienced the triumph of free will. How did you exercise self-control and overcome impulses or desires? What were the outcomes of these moments of self-mastery?

- Reflect on the relationship between passion and leadership. Do you agree with Gracián's assertion that those ruled by passion should avoid aiming for high office? How might emotional detachment contribute to effective leadership?

- Think about situations where emotional detachment and self-control could have avoided scandals or damaged reputations. How might applying these principles have altered the outcome of these situations?

- Consider that emotional detachment is the shortest way back to a good reputation. Have you ever experienced a situation where restoring your reputation required you to detach from strong emotions or impulses? How did you navigate this process?

- Reflect on your journey towards emotional mastery and self-control. What strategies have you found effective in managing your impulses and passions? How do you envision continuing to cultivate these qualities in the future?

So vital is mastery of self,

To maintain one's status and wealth.

A privilege rare, for the mind so bold,

To be without passions, a treasure untold.

―――

My Dearest Friend,

One must heed the wisdom of mastering the passions in pursuing power and influence. It is a privilege of the highest order of mind to transcend the whims of transient impulses and base desires. By attaining such mastery, we elevate ourselves above the common fray, demonstrating our strength of character and clarity of purpose.

While a driving force for many, passion can be a double-edged sword in politics and power. Those governed by their emotions are prone to erratic behavior and vulnerable to scandal. We must exercise restraint and discipline over our impulses to avoid such pitfalls, for it is the path to maintaining a sterling reputation and securing our place in the annals of history.

Aspiring leaders must recognize that passion can cloud judgment and hinder our ascent to greatness. Instead, we must strive for a refined sense of control, for it is the only way to navigate the treacherous waters of political intrigue and social dynamics. By mastering ourselves, we gain the respect and admiration of our peers, paving the way for success in our endeavors.

Let us not be swayed by the allure of momentary pleasures or the temptation of fleeting desires. Instead, let us embrace the triumph of free will and exercise prudence in all our actions, for it is through self-control and rationality that we distinguish ourselves from the masses and emerge as true leaders among men.

With steadfast determination and unwavering resolve, we shall rise above the tumult of passion and carve out our place in the annals of history.

Yours faithfully,

Niccolò Machiavelli

STRATEGIES

Master Self-Control: Practice discipline and restraint over your impulses and emotions. Keep a cool head in all situations, avoiding impulsive actions or emotional outbursts.

Aim Low: Avoid seeking high office if you cannot control your passions, as it will only lead to scandal and downfall.

Embrace Detachment: Cultivate a sense of detachment from transient desires and low impulses.

Prioritize Reputation: Recognize that a good reputation is invaluable and prioritize actions that uphold it. Steer clear of situations that may lead to scandal or tarnish your reputation.

Exercise Free Will: Assert your free will by refusing to be governed by fleeting emotions or desires.

Strive for Excellence: Aspire to the highest order of mind by transcending base impulses and achieving self-mastery.

Choose Discretion: Practice discretion, especially personal desires or passions.

Focus on Virtue: Embrace virtuous behavior and cultivate a reputation for integrity and moral uprightness.

Be Strategic: Plan your actions carefully, considering the potential consequences on your reputation and standing.

Cultivate Dignity: Present yourself with dignity and poise, projecting an image of strength and self-control.

Learn from Mistakes: Reflect on past errors and strive to learn from them, improving your ability to navigate future challenges.

Surround Yourself Wisely: Associate with individuals who exhibit self-mastery and moral fortitude, learning from their example.

Since reputation and integrity hold powerful sway.

It's smart to let virtue guide your way.

Choose on discretion in every deed -

And don't be driven by your base needs.

9 - AVOID THE FAULTS OF YOUR NATION

Avoid the Faults of your Nation | Water shares the good or bad qualities of the strata through which it flows, and man those of the climate in which he is born. Some owe more than others to their native land because the zenith has a more favorable sky. No nation, even among the most civilized, does not have some fault peculiar to itself that other nations blame by boasting or as a warning. 'Tis a triumph of cleverness to correct in oneself such national failings, or even to hide them: you get great credit for being unique among your fellows, and as it is less expected of you, it is esteemed the more. There are also family failings and position, office, or age faults. If these all meet in one person and are not carefully guarded against, they make an intolerable monster.

The analogy between water and man's qualities suggests that just as water takes on the characteristics of the strata through which it flows, man's traits are shaped by the environment in which he is born. Some individuals owe more to their native land due to favorable conditions, much like a more favorable climate can nurture certain qualities.

Gracián highlights that no nation, however civilized, is without faults, which may be peculiar to itself. These faults are often subject to criticism from other nations, either as a form of boast or as a cautionary tale. However, it is considered a triumph of cleverness to recognize and correct these national failings within oneself or to conceal them altogether. In doing so, one earns praise for standing out among peers and defying expectations.

Furthermore, Gracián acknowledges the existence of family failings, as well as faults stemming from one's position, office, or age. When these traits converge in an individual without proper vigilance, they can create an intolerable amalgamation of flaws.

Gracián underscores the importance of self-awareness and self-improvement in overcoming the inherent faults associated with one's origin, upbringing, or circumstances. By recognizing and addressing these shortcomings, individuals can distinguish themselves and earn admiration for their ability to rise above societal norms and expectations. Additionally, by guarding against the convergence of multiple faults, one can avoid becoming an insufferable embodiment of flaws.

REFLECTIONS

- Reflect on the unique cultural or societal traits associated with your nationality. How do these characteristics influence your identity and behavior?

- Consider whether there are any stereotypes or generalizations about your nationality that you believe hold. How do these perceptions affect your interactions with others?

- Think about your family background and upbringing. Are there any specific family traits or tendencies you have inherited or observed? How do these characteristics contribute to your sense of self?

- Reflect on your faults or shortcomings. Do any of these align with broader national or cultural stereotypes? How do you navigate these aspects of yourself in various social settings?

- Consider the concept of self-improvement and personal development. How might you work to overcome or mitigate any negative traits associated with your nationality or upbringing?

- Explore the idea of individuality within a cultural context. How can embracing your unique qualities while acknowledging cultural influences help you navigate diverse social environments?

- Reflect on the notion of societal expectations and norms. How do these expectations influence your behavior, and how might you challenge or redefine them in pursuit of personal growth?

- Explore the concept of tolerance and empathy towards individuals from different cultural backgrounds. How can recognizing and appreciating diversity contribute to personal and societal harmony?

As water shares traits from whence it flows,

So man inherits qualities from where he arose.

GUARD AGAINST THE MONSTER WITHIN,

Lest it rise up, and lead to sin.

———

My Dearest Friend,

In our world, much like water, we carry the qualities of the environment in which we are born. Just as water takes on the characteristics of the strata through which it flows, we inherit the faults and virtues of our nation, family, and social position.

Yet, it is not enough to merely accept these faults as inevitable. No, my friend, it is the mark of genuine cleverness to recognize and correct the shortcomings of our upbringing. By doing so, we distinguish ourselves from our peers and earn admiration for our adaptability and ingenuity.

But heed my words: while it may be necessary to conceal these faults at times, it is equally important not to allow them to converge within us. The convergence of multiple faults in one individual can lead to disaster, transforming them into what I can only describe as an "intolerable monster."

Therefore, my friend, I urge you to be strategic in your approach. Guard against the negative influences of your environment and manage perceptions of your character with utmost care. In doing so, you will position yourself for success in the complex web of human relationships and power dynamics.

Remember, it is not enough to be a product of our environment. We must rise above it, using our wit and cunning to shape our destiny. You will easily navigate these challenges with your intelligence and foresight.

Yours faithfully,

Niccolò Machiavelli

STRATEGIES

Study Your Environment: Analyze the cultural, social, and political landscape in which you operate to understand the prevailing norms and expectations.

Identify National and Cultural Faults: Recognize the inherent flaws and virtues of your nation, family, and social position.

Conceal or Correct Faults: Determine whether it is more advantageous to conceal your inherited faults or to address and correct them to your advantage.

Adaptability and Ingenuity: Demonstrate adaptability and ingenuity by correcting or concealing faults to distinguish yourself from your peers.

Strategic Concealment: Conceal faults strategically, only revealing them when necessary or advantageous.

Guard Against Convergence of Faults: Be vigilant in guarding against the convergence of multiple faults within yourself, which can lead to personal or professional disaster.

Maintain a Positive Image: Manage perceptions of your character carefully to maintain a positive image and reputation.

Navigate Power Dynamics: Understand power dynamics and relationships within your environment to navigate them effectively.

Use Wit and Cunning: Employ your intelligence, wit, and cunning to shape your destiny and achieve your goals.

Position for Success: Position yourself for success by leveraging your understanding of your environment, adapting to circumstances, and capitalizing on opportunities.

To navigate well, one must learn

The social and political norms to discern.

Study carefully the culture and laws

To highlight virtues and manage flaws.

10 - FORTUNE AND FAME

Fortune and Fame | Where the one is fickle, the other is enduring. The first for life, the second afterward; the one against envy, the other against oblivion. Fortune is desired, at times assisted; fame is earned. The desire for fame springs from man's best part. It was and is the sister of the giants; it always goes to extremes—horrible monsters or brilliant prodigies.

Fortune and Fame encapsulate two distinct yet intertwined concepts in human aspiration and achievement. While Fortune is characterized by its fickleness, constantly shifting and elusive, Fame stands as a beacon of enduring recognition and admiration.

With its erratic nature, Fortune offers fleeting rewards and benefits during one's lifetime. It is often desired and sometimes assisted through strategic actions or endeavors. However, its transience leaves individuals vulnerable to envy and the whims of fate. In contrast, Fame transcends the limitations of time, offering a form of immortality long after one's passing. It serves as a shield against oblivion, ensuring one's legacy endures beyond the confines of mortal existence.

The desire for Fame originates from the noblest aspects of human nature, springing from the innate yearning for recognition and significance. It is a pursuit that resonates with the essence of humanity, driving individuals to strive for greatness and leave a lasting impact on the world.

Throughout history, Fame has been associated with extremes, aligning itself with horrific monsters or brilliant prodigies. It is a force that knows no moderation, propelling individuals to the highest peak of achievement or plunging them into infamy. Yet, despite its unpredictable nature, the allure of Fame remains irresistible, beckoning individuals to pursue greatness at any cost.

While Fortune may offer temporary blessings and boons, Fame genuinely captures the essence of human ambition and aspiration. Pursuing lasting recognition and legacy drives individuals to push the boundaries of human potential and leave an indelible mark on the tapestry of history.

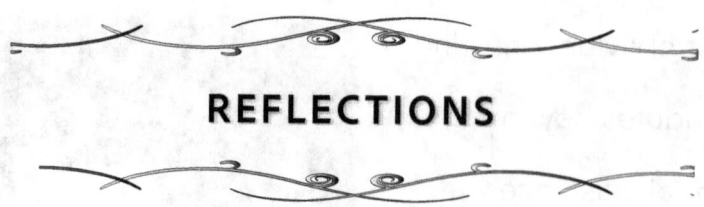

REFLECTIONS

- Reflect on a time when you experienced the fickleness of fortune in your own life. How did this experience shape your perspective on the transient nature of material wealth or success?

- Consider individuals or figures from history who have achieved enduring fame. What qualities or actions do you believe contributed to their lasting legacy? How does their example inspire you in your pursuit of recognition or significance?

- Explore the concept of envy and its role in both fortune and fame. Have you ever felt envious of someone else's success or recognition? How did you navigate these feelings, and what insights did you gain from the experience?

- Reflect on the distinction between desiring fortune versus earning fame. Have you ever pursued recognition or acclaim for its own sake without considering the hard work or merit required to achieve it? How do you approach the pursuit of fame in a way that aligns with your values and principles?

- Think about the origins of your desire for fame or recognition. What drives this desire, and how does it reflect your aspirations and ideals? How do you channel this desire into productive and meaningful pursuits?

- Consider the metaphor of fame as the sister of the giants, always going to extremes. Have you ever observed individuals who achieved fame but faced challenges or struggles? How does this idea inform your understanding of the complexities and nuances of achieving recognition?

- Reflect on your relationship with fortune and fame. How do you balance pursuing material success with seeking lasting recognition or legacy? What lessons or insights have you gained from navigating these dual aspirations?

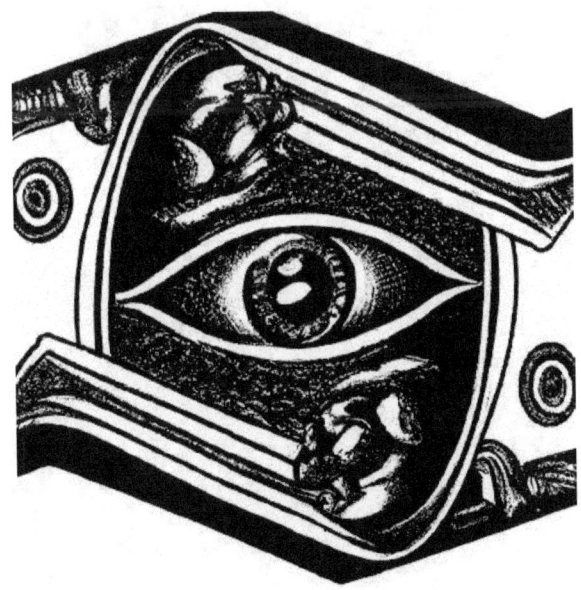

FORTUNE, FLEETING, HER FAVOR FLIES,

ONE MOMENT HIGH, THE NEXT DENIES.

BUT FAME, THE STALWART, STANDS THE TEST,

AGAINST OBLIVION'S COLD, RELENTLESS QUEST.

———

My Dear Friend,

In contemplating the nature of fortune and fame, I am reminded of the profound implications these concepts hold for those who seek power and influence in the world. With its capriciousness and transience, Fortune represents the unpredictable nature of life's circumstances. It is a fleeting force that can bring temporary success and material wealth but should not be relied upon as the sole determinant of greatness.

On the other hand, fame endures beyond one's lifetime, serving as a lasting legacy that transcends the ephemeral nature of fortune. Fame is earned through sustained effort, achievement, and cultivating a positive reputation. It reflects noble aspirations and the desire for lasting recognition in the annals of history.

We must recognize the distinction between fortune and fame in our pursuit of greatness. While fortune may offer temporary advantages, fame ensures a lasting impact and a place in the annals of history. Therefore, it is wise to prioritize the pursuit of fame over the transient allure of fortune.

One must embody wisdom, prudence, and strategic foresight to achieve lasting fame. By cultivating a positive reputation through virtuous conduct and calculated actions, one can secure enduring influence and admiration from others.

In conclusion, let us heed the lessons of history and strive for lasting fame rather than relying solely on the uncertainties of fortune. By understanding the distinction between these concepts and strategically pursuing fame through virtuous conduct and calculated actions, we can secure a lasting legacy that will endure for generations.

Yours faithfully,

Niccolò Machiavelli

STRATEGIES

Strategic Planning & Public Relations: Develop a long-term plan to cultivate fame rather than relying solely on short-term fortune. Engage in strategic communication and public relations efforts to shape public perception and enhance your reputation.

Virtuous Conduct & Reputation: Embody virtues such as wisdom, prudence, and strategic foresight to earn lasting admiration. Focus on building a positive reputation through calculated actions and virtuous behavior.

Avoid Dependency on Fortune: Do not rely solely on luck or external circumstances for success; prioritize actions leading to enduring fame.

Strategic Alliances: Form alliances and partnerships with influential individuals or groups to enhance your reputation and increase your sphere of influence.

Adaptability: Be flexible and adaptable in your approach, adjusting strategies as circumstances change to maintain a positive trajectory toward lasting fame.

Learn from History: Study the successes and failures of historical figures to glean insights into practical strategies for achieving enduring fame.

Symbolism and Image: Use symbolism and carefully crafted images to enhance your reputation and create a lasting legacy.

Strategic Communication: Utilize strategic communication tactics to control the narrative surrounding your actions and achievements.

Long-Term Perspective: Maintain a long-term perspective, understanding that enduring fame requires sustained effort and strategic planning over time.

PUBLIC RELATIONS, THE VITAL ART,

SHAPES PERCEPTION AS WE PLAY OUR PART.

AN IMAGE AND NARRATIVE CAREFULLY SPUN

ENHANCE OUR LEGACY WHEN ALL IS DONE.

11 - CULTIVATE THOSE WHO CAN TEACH YOU

Cultivate those who can teach you. Let friendly intercourse be a school of knowledge, and culture be taught through conversation. Thus, you make your friends your teachers and mingle the pleasures of conversation with the advantages of instruction. Sensible persons thus enjoy alternating pleasures: they reap applause for what they say and gain instruction from what they hear. We are always attracted to others by our interests, but in this case, it is higher. Wise men frequent the houses of great noblemen not because they are temples of vanity but as theaters of good breeding. Some gentlemen have the credit of worldly wisdom because they are not only oracles of all nobleness by their example and behavior but also because those who surround them form a well-bred academy of worldly wisdom of the best and noblest kind.

To cultivate those who can teach you is to recognize the immense value of learning from others. Friendly interaction is a fertile ground for acquiring knowledge, where conversations become classrooms and culture is imparted through dialogue. By embracing this approach, one transforms friends into mentors, blending the joys of conversation with the benefits of instruction.

In this mutually enriching exchange, sensible individuals delight in sharing their insights and absorbing wisdom from others. They bask in the applause for their contributions while humbly embracing the opportunity to learn from their peers.

The allure of such interactions transcends mere self-interest; it is rooted in a deeper appreciation for intellectual growth and refinement. Wise individuals seek out the company of the learned not for vanity's sake but as environments where good manners and etiquette thrive.

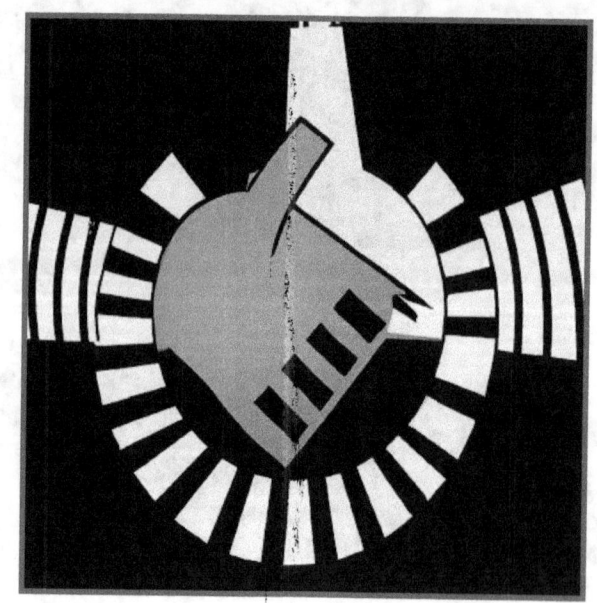

In the noble pursuit of worldly wisdom, certain gentlemen and noble figures stand as paragons. They embody virtues through their actions and foster an atmosphere of intellectual stimulation among their associates. Their households become academies of refinement, where the finest principles of worldly wisdom are imparted and upheld.

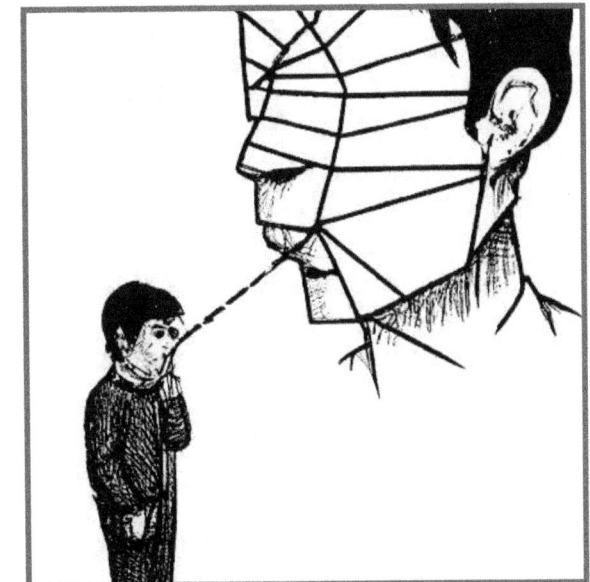

Ultimately, to cultivate those who can teach you is to recognize the inherent richness of human interaction. Through these exchanges, we expand our horizons, deepen our understanding, and refine our character, ensuring that the pursuit of knowledge remains a lifelong endeavor enriched by the companionship of fellow seekers.

REFLECTIONS

- Consider the role of friendship in your life. How do your friends influence your intellectual and cultural pursuits? Are there specific individuals who serve as mentors or sources of inspiration for you?

- Think about occasions when you've reaped both applause and instruction from conversations. What topics or discussions tend to evoke this dual pleasure for you? How do you balance sharing your insights and learning from others?

- Reflect on your motivations for seeking out certain individuals as companions. Are there specific qualities or traits you value in your friends or mentors? How do these relationships contribute to your overall well-being and personal development?

- Consider the concept of "good breeding," as the passage mentions. What does it mean to you, and how do you cultivate it in your interactions with others? Are there particular environments or social circles where you feel a sense of refinement and intellectual stimulation?

- Reflect on the influence of wise individuals in your life. Have you observed specific individuals who embody worldly wisdom through their actions and behavior? How have they contributed to shaping your values and principles?

- Explore ways you can further cultivate relationships with individuals who can teach you. Are there steps you can take to foster deeper intellectual and cultural exchanges with your friends and acquaintances? How can you make friendly intercourse a more enriching experience for both yourself and others?

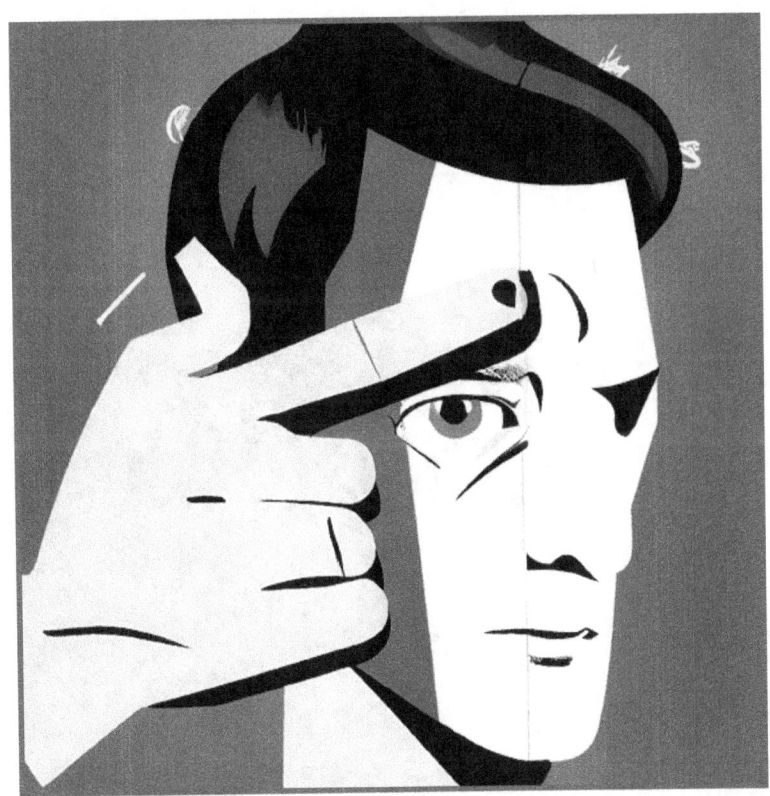

IN FRIENDLY DISCOURSE, LET KNOWLEDGE FLOW,

A SCHOOL OF THOUGHT WHERE MINDS CAN GROW.

FOR IN CONVERSATION'S GENTLE EMBRACE,

LIES THE PATH TO WISDOM'S GRACE.

———

My Dearest Friend,

Allow me to impart some Machiavellian wisdom that has withstood the test of time. We must cultivate relationships with knowledgeable and influential individuals in our pursuit of greatness. These wise and influential figures serve as invaluable sources of insight and guidance, allowing us to expand our understanding and advance our ambitions.

Engaging in friendly discourse and conversation with such individuals is not merely a means of intellectual enrichment but also a strategic maneuver to elevate our status and reputation. By associating ourselves with the learned and noble, we project an image of sophistication and intelligence, garnering respect and admiration from our peers.

Moreover, aligning ourselves with influential figures, such as great noblemen, gives us a distinct advantage in navigating the intricate web of politics and social dynamics. By demonstrating loyalty and deference to these influential individuals, we secure their favor and protection, ensuring our position of influence and security in the world.

Pursuing knowledge and cultivating influential relationships are not mutually exclusive endeavors but complementary aspects of our journey toward greatness. By embracing the wisdom of others and strategically aligning ourselves with those in positions of power, we pave the way for our success and prosperity.

I urge you to heed these words and take deliberate action in cultivating relationships with those who can teach you. Remember, in the pursuit of greatness, every alliance and every conversation is an opportunity to further our ambitions and secure our place in the annals of history.

With warm regards,

Niccolò Machiavelli

STRATEGIES

Identify influential individuals: Identify individuals who possess knowledge, influence, and power in various spheres of society.

Build relationships: Cultivate relationships with these influential individuals through friendly discourse and conversation.

Demonstrate deference: Show respect and deference to those in positions of power and authority to secure their favor and protection.

Seek mentorship: Seek mentorship from wise and experienced individuals who can offer guidance and insight into navigating the complexities of life and society.

Align with the powerful: Align yourself strategically with individuals who hold significant sway in political, social, or economic circles to bolster your influence and status.

Leverage social connections: Utilize your social connections and networks to access valuable opportunities and resources.

Display loyalty: Demonstrate loyalty and allegiance to those who can further your interests and ambitions while remaining adaptable to changing circumstances.

Maintain discretion: Exercise discretion in your interactions and conversations, revealing only as much as necessary to cultivate intrigue and maintain control over your image and reputation.

Learn from others: Continuously seek to learn from the wisdom and experiences of others, recognizing that knowledge is a powerful tool in the pursuit of greatness.

Adapt to circumstances: Be flexible and adaptable in your approach, adjusting your strategies and tactics to navigate the ever-changing landscape of human interaction and politics.

ABSORBING WISDOM IS AN ESSENTIAL PART

OF SKILLFULLY PRACTICING OUR STRATEGIC ART.

FOR PRIVILEGE AND OPPORTUNITIES TO AMASS,

ASSEMBLE A NETWORK BOTH WISE AND VAST.

12 - NATURE AND ART

Nature and Art: material and artistry. There is no beauty unadorned and no excellence that would not become barbaric if it were not supported by artifice: this remedies the evil and improves the good. Nature scarcely gives us the very best; we must recourse to art. Without this, the best natural dispositions are uncultured; half lack excellence if training is absent. Everyone has something unpolished without artificial training, and every kind of excellence needs some polish.

ature and art are complementary forces in beauty and excellence, embodying the duality of material and artistry. While nature provides the raw materials, art refines and enhances them, elevating them to their fullest potential.

In its unadorned state, natural beauty may be raw and untamed, lacking the refinement and sophistication that artifice can provide. Conversely, even the most exceptional natural qualities may appear crude and primitive without the guiding hand of artistry to shape and polish them.

Art is a remedy for natural deficiencies, smoothing rough edges and highlighting inherent virtues. Through skill and craftsmanship, artifice transforms the ordinary into the extraordinary, enhancing beauty and excellence in all its forms.

Moreover, the relationship between nature and art underscores the importance of cultivation and training in pursuing excellence. While nature may provide a foundation, it is through deliberate effort and artistic intervention that true greatness is achieved. Without the guiding hand of art, even the most promising natural dispositions remain uncultivated and incomplete.

Indeed, every individual possesses unpolished aspects and needs

refinement, just as every form of excellence requires the touch of artistry to reach its full potential. Through the marriage of nature and art, we harness the power of raw materials and skilled craftsmanship to create beauty, excellence, and sophistication in all aspects of life.

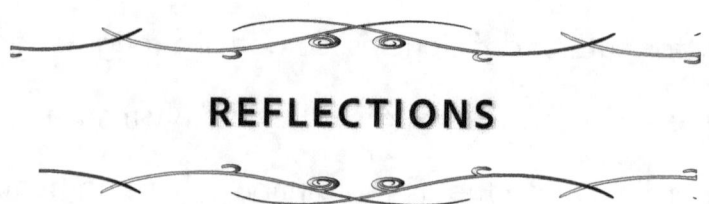

REFLECTIONS

- Reflect on instances where you've witnessed the interplay between natural abilities and cultivated skills. How has combining innate talent and deliberate practice contributed to personal growth or success?

- Consider examples from history, literature, or art where individuals or societies have exemplified the principles of enhancing natural beauty or excellence through artifice. What lessons can be drawn from these examples?

- Explore areas of your life where you perceive untapped potential or unrefined abilities. How might you apply the concept of deception to refine these qualities and unlock more significant levels of excellence?

- Contemplate the idea that nature rarely provides the very best without art intervention. How does this notion resonate with your experiences or observations of the world?

- Think about the role of education, training, and deliberate practice in shaping personal development and achievement. How have you seen the impact of intentional effort in enhancing natural talents or abilities?

- Consider the balance between embracing natural qualities and actively cultivating them through deception. Are there areas where you lean too heavily on one aspect over the other? How might you achieve a more harmonious integration of nature and art in your pursuits?

- Reflect on the significance of polish and refinement in various aspects of life, such as relationships, careers, hobbies, or personal development. How can attention to detail and deliberate practice contribute to excellence in these areas?

NATURE'S BOUNTY AND ART'S DESIGN

YOU MUST HONOR BOTH IN KIND,

FOR IN THEIR UNION, WE SEE,

THE TRUEST FORM OF HARMONY.

My Dearest Friend,

I trust this letter finds you well and in good spirits. Allow me to impart some wisdom that I have gleaned from my experiences and observations.

Nature and Art, my friend, are two sides of the same coin in pursuing greatness. While nature provides us with inherent abilities and qualities, it is through deception and strategic manipulation that we refine and amplify these traits to achieve our objectives.

In politics and power, more is needed to rely solely on our natural talents. We must employ cunning and deception to shape public perception and gain the upper hand. Just as a skilled artist can transform raw materials into a masterpiece, so can we manipulate our circumstances to achieve our goals.

Consider this: nature seldom provides us with the very best. We enhance our natural dispositions through cunning and training and reach our full potential. Every individual has areas that require polishing, and we address these shortcomings through strategic maneuvering and calculated actions.

Therefore, my friend, I urge you to embrace the art of manipulation and craftiness. Cultivate your natural talents, but do not rely on them alone. Seek out knowledge and education to supplement your abilities, and always appreciate the power of strategic action.

Remember, it is not enough to possess natural talents; we must also possess the cunning and deception to leverage them effectively. By mastering the delicate balance between nature and art, we can achieve greatness and secure our place in the annals of history.

Yours in wisdom,

Niccolò Machiavelli

STRATEGIES

Embrace Artifice: Utilize cunning and strategic manipulation to refine and amplify natural talents and qualities.

Continuous Improvement: Seek learning opportunities to supplement innate abilities and acquire additional skills. Recognize that nature seldom provides the best; strive for constant refinement and enhancement through training and education.

Polish Natural Dispositions: Identify areas that require improvement and apply strategic methods to address shortcomings.

Balance Nature and Art: Maintain a delicate equilibrium between natural talents and strategic manipulation to maximize effectiveness.

Master the Art of Manipulation: Learn to influence others and shape perceptions to achieve desired outcomes. Employ calculated actions and maneuvers to shape circumstances and achieve desired outcomes.

BALANCING NATURE AND ART ARE KEY TO SUCCEED

SO PERPETUAL IMPROVEMENT IS OUR GUIDING CREED.

FOR BEAUTY AND EXCELLENCE, HAND IN HAND,

ARE BORN OF NATURE'S SOIL, BUT REFINED VIA ART'S COMMAND.

13 - ACT SOMETIMES ON SECOND THOUGHTS, SOMETIMES ON FIRST IMPULSE.

Act sometimes on second thoughts, sometimes on first impulse. I Man's life is a warfare against the malice of men. Sagacity fights with strategic changes of intention: it never does what it threatens; it aims only at escaping notice. It aims dexterously in the air and strikes home in an unexpected direction, always seeking to conceal its game. It lets a purpose appear to attract the opponent's attention but then turns around and conquers by the unexpected. But a penetrating intelligence anticipates this by watchfulness and lurks in ambush. It always understands the opposite of what the opponent wishes it to understand and recognizes every feint of guile. It lets the first impulse pass by and waits for the second or third. Sagacity now rises to higher flights on seeing its artifice foreseen and tries to deceive by truth itself, changes its game to change its deceit, cheats by not cheating, and finds deception on the most extraordinary candor. But the opposing intelligence is on guard with increased watchfulness, discovers the darkness concealed by the light, and deciphers every move, the more subtle because more simple. In this way, the guile of Python combats the far-darting rays of Apollo.

This aphorism encapsulates the intricate dance of strategic maneuvering and cunning intelligence in the battleground of life. Human existence is likened to a constant warfare against the hostility of others, where sagacity emerges as the weapon of choice, wielding strategic changes of intention like a seasoned warrior.

Sagacity, characterized by its keen insight and cleverness, operates with finesse and subtlety. It strategically feints and maneuvers, never executing what it threatens but aiming to evade detection. Like a skilled archer, it aims in the air precisely, striking unexpectedly and concealing its true intentions.

However, penetrating intelligence anticipates these tactics, lurking in ambush and deciphering every feint of guile. It patiently waits, allowing the first impulse to pass and discerning the true motives behind every move. As sagacity attempts to deceive with truth, the opposing intelligence remains vigilant, detecting the darkness concealed by apparent honesty.

The battle between sagacity and intelligence is a relentless struggle of wits, where each seeks to outmaneuver the other. Yet, even as sagacity attempts to deceive by not cheating, the opposing intelligence rises to the challenge,

deciphering the most subtle moves with unwavering clarity.

In this intricate dance of deception and detection, the guile of sagacity clashes with the sharp discernment of intelligence, akin to the legendary battle between the Python and the far-darting rays of

Apollo. Each side employs its arsenal of tactics, navigating the complexities of human interaction with skill and precision.

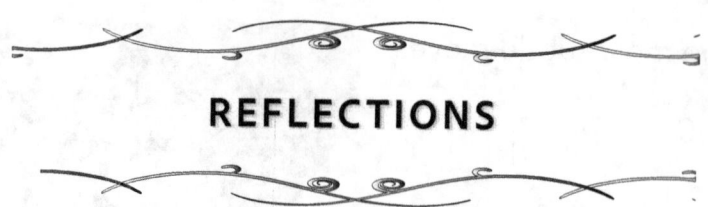

REFLECTIONS

- Reflect on when you had to navigate a situation where strategic thinking and quick decision-making were crucial. How did you approach the challenge? Did you find yourself acting on the first impulse, or did you take a moment to consider your options before acting?

- Consider instances in your life where you've encountered individuals who exhibited sagacity or penetrating intelligence in their interactions with others. How did you perceive their behavior? Did you recognize their tactics in navigating social dynamics and conflicts?

- Explore the concept of warfare as a metaphor for life's challenges and conflicts. How do you view the idea that man's life is a constant battle against the malice of others? Have you experienced situations where you felt you were in a symbolic battle with someone else's ill intentions?

- Reflect on the role of deception and cunning in interpersonal interactions. Have you ever encountered situations where someone attempted to deceive you or where you had to navigate complex social dynamics with strategic changes of intention? How did you respond?

- Think about your approach to decision-making and problem-solving. Are you more inclined to act on the first impulse, or do you tend to wait for second or third thoughts before moving? How do you think this approach influences your interactions with others?

- Consider the balance between honesty and deceit in social interactions. Have you ever experienced situations where someone attempted to deceive you using the truth itself? How did you respond to this tactic, and what insights did you gain from the experience?

- Reflect on the metaphor of the Python combating the far-darting rays of Apollo. How does this imagery resonate with your understanding of the interplay between deception and detection in human interactions?

CUNNING AND INTELLIGENCE ENTWINE,

AND GUIDE OUR PLOTS IN A GRAND DESIGN.

THE PURPOSE APPARENT? A MERE RUSE TO ENSNARE

FOES BEGUILED ARE CAUGHT UNAWARE.

———

My Dearest Companion,

In the grand theater of life, where every moment presents a new challenge and every interaction a potential battlefield, sagacity reigns supreme as the weapon of choice for those who seek to navigate the treacherous waters of human affairs. I am pleased to share my reflections on strategic maneuvering, a skill that has served me well in my endeavors and will prove invaluable to you.

Sagacity, my dear friend, is the cornerstone of success in our ongoing warfare against the malice of men. The keenness of mind allows us to anticipate our adversaries' moves and discern their intentions even as they seek to conceal them. It is the art of acting sometimes on second thoughts, sometimes on first impulse, to confound our opponents and achieve our objectives through deception and misdirection.

As we navigate the complexities of human interaction, we must recognize that our adversaries are constantly watching, waiting for any sign of weakness or vulnerability. Therefore, we must cultivate an air of unpredictability, letting our purpose appear only to vanish in the next moment and deceive by truth itself, founding our deception on the most extraordinary candor.

But let us not forget that our adversaries are not the only ones capable of deception. We, too, must be vigilant, always on guard against the darkness concealed by the light, deciphering every move with the utmost care and attention.

In closing, my dear friend, remember that sagacity is not merely a skill to master but a way of life. By embracing the art of strategic maneuvering, we can navigate the complexities of human interaction with skill and finesse, achieving our goals while outsmarting our adversaries at every turn.

Yours in cunning and deception,

Niccolò Machiavelli

STRATEGIES

Strategic Maneuvering: Employ strategic intention changes to confound adversaries and achieve objectives through deception and misdirection. Remain on guard to discover the darkness concealed by the light. Decipher every move, no matter how subtle, to outmaneuver opponents.

Concealment of Intentions: Aim to escape notice by concealing your true intentions. Let a purpose attract attention, then turn around and conquer the unexpected.

Patience and Timing: Let the first impulse pass by and wait for the second or third before taking action. On seeing your artifice foreseen, rise to higher flights of sagacity and adapt your strategy accordingly.

Deception through Truth: Deceive by the truth itself, changing your game to change your deceit. Found deception on the most extraordinary openness to enhance its effectiveness.

Flexibility and Adaptability: Be prepared to change tactics and strategies as the situation evolves. Adapt to new circumstances to maintain the upper hand and secure victory.

Unpredictability: Cultivate an air of unpredictability to keep adversaries off balance. Mix strategic changes with calculated risks to maintain the element of surprise.

Keen Observation: Pay close attention to the behaviors and motivations of others. Use this information to anticipate their actions and manipulate situations to your advantage.

Mastery of Timing: Develop a keen sense of timing to seize opportunities and exploit vulnerabilities. Strike at the right moment to achieve maximum impact and secure your objectives.

STRATEGIC MANEUVERING IS KEY,

TO CONFOUND OUR FOES AND SECURE OUR VICTORY.

APPEARANCES DECEIVE WHEN LITTLE IS DISPLAYED,

SO IT'S EASY TO TURN THE TABLES WITH A MOVE WELL PLAYED.

The Thing Itself and the Way It Is Done | "Substance" is not enough: "accident" is also required, as the scholastics say. A destructive manner spoils everything, even reason and justice; a good one supplies everything, gilds a No, sweetens a truth, and adds a touch of beauty to old age itself. The show plays a large part in affairs; a suitable manner steals into the affection. Acceptable behavior is a joy in life, and a pleasant expression helps out of a difficulty in a remarkable way.

This section underscores the importance of both substance and manner in human interactions. While substance provides the foundation, how something is done shapes perceptions and impacts outcomes.

More than merely possessing substance or material wealth is required; how these are presented and executed truly matters. Scholars recognize that "substance" and "accident" are necessary components, implying that the mere existence of something is not enough; the appropriate presentation or manner must also accompany it.

The significance of manner becomes particularly apparent in social interactions and communication. A lousy manner can tarnish even the most rational argument or cause, while a good one can enhance and elevate even the most challenging situations. Manners can transform a negative response into a more palatable experience, sweetening the truth and adding a touch of grace to difficult conversations.

Moreover, how actions are carried out can significantly influence how others receive them. Good behavior and refined manners can win over hearts and forge strong connections with others. A pleasant expression or demeanor can be a beacon of light, quickly guiding individuals through challenges and difficulties.

Ultimately, acceptable behavior and pleasant manners are desirable qualities and essential tools for navigating the complexities of life. In this way, how things are done holds significant sway over the outcomes we experience in our personal and professional lives.

REFLECTIONS

- Consider moments in your life where you've experienced the effects of good or bad manners firsthand. How did these experiences shape your perceptions of the individuals involved? Did you find yourself more inclined to trust or sympathize with those who exhibited good manners?

- Explore the concept of "accident" about substance. How do you interpret that more than just substance is required for success or effectiveness? Can you think of examples from your own life where how something was presented or executed made a significant difference?

- Reflect on the impact of good manners on various aspects of life, such as relationships, work, and personal well-being. How have you observed acceptable behavior contributing to joy and harmony in your interactions with others? Have you ever experienced a situation where a pleasant expression or demeanor helped resolve a difficulty?

- Consider the role of manners in society and culture. How do cultural norms and expectations influence how manners are perceived and practiced? Do specific cultural practices or traditions related to manners resonate with you?

- Reflect on your behavior and manners. Are there areas where you could improve how you present yourself and interact with others? How might cultivating good manners enhance your relationships and overall quality of life?

- Imagine a scenario where you are faced with a challenging situation. How might applying good manners and exemplary behavior help you navigate this difficulty gracefully and effectively? What strategies could you employ to ensure that your handling of the situation contributes positively to the outcome?

"THE THING ITSELF" IS NOT ALL THAT'S KNOWN -

IT ALSO MATTERS HOW THE DEED IS SHOWN,

SO REMEMBER, DEAR FRIEND, IN ALL THAT YOU DO,

THE THING ITSELF, AND THE WAY IT'S DONE, TOO.

My Dear Friend,

Allow me to impart Machiavellian wisdom regarding the importance of "the thing itself" and "the way it is done." As scholars often say, substance alone is insufficient; we must also consider how our actions are carried out.

Consider this: even the most righteous or rational actions can be tarnished by a bad manner or demeanor. In the intricate dance of politics and social interactions, presentation matters greatly. A suitable manner, on the other hand, can elevate even the simplest of actions, making them more palatable and effective.

In our quest for success, we must understand that exemplary behavior and pleasant expressions are not mere luxuries but strategic tools. They can sway opinions, win allies, and diffuse tensions. By mastering the art of presentation and demeanor, we can navigate the complexities of human interactions with more remarkable finesse and achieve our objectives more effectively.

Remember, my friend, that appearances often matter as much as substance in politics and power. By paying attention to "the thing itself" and "the way it is done," we can increase our influence, manipulate perceptions, and secure our position in the world.

Yours faithfully,

Niccolò Machiavelli

STRATEGIES

Use pleasant expressions strategically: Employ a friendly and approachable demeanor when dealing with others, especially in challenging situations. A pleasant expression can help to disarm potential adversaries and pave the way for smoother negotiations or interactions.

Sweeten the truth: When delivering difficult or unfavorable news, temper it with tact and diplomacy. Find ways to present the information that softens its impact without compromising its essence. This can help to maintain goodwill and avoid unnecessary conflict.

Add a touch of beauty to your actions: Seek opportunities to enhance the aesthetic appeal of your endeavors. Whether through well-designed presentations, eloquent speeches, or thoughtful gestures, adding a touch of beauty to your actions can captivate and inspire those around you.

Recognize the importance of exemplary behavior: Understand that good manners and etiquette are not merely social niceties but strategic assets. Cultivate a reputation for impeccable behavior, as this can earn you respect, admiration, and loyalty from others.

Adapt your demeanor to different contexts: Recognize that how you present yourself may need to vary depending on the situation and the individuals involved. Adapt your demeanor and behavior accordingly to maximize your effectiveness in different settings.

Invest in your presentation: Take the time to cultivate a polished and professional image. Pay attention to your appearance, grooming, and body language, as these factors can significantly influence how others perceive you and your actions.

LET YOUR INTERACTIONS BE WISE,

YOUR PRESENTATION IS THE GUISE.

IMPECCABLE MANNERS, A POLISHED SHEEN,

WILL ALWAYS REIGN SOCIALLY SUPREME.

15 - KEEP MINISTERING SPIRITS

Keep Ministering Spirits | It is a privilege of the mighty to surround themselves with the champions of intellect; these extricate them from every fear of ignorance, and these worry out for them the moot points of every difficulty. 'Tis a rare greatness to use the wise and far exceeds the vicious taste of Tigranes, who fancied captive monarchs as his servants. It is a novel kind of supremacy, the best that life can offer, to have as servants by skill those who by nature are our masters. 'Tis a great thing to know, little to live: no real life without knowledge. There is remarkable cleverness in studying without study, in getting much using many, and through them all to become wise. Afterward, you speak in the council chamber on behalf of many, and as many sages speak through your mouth as were consulted beforehand: you thus obtain the fame of an oracle by others' toil. Such ministering spirits distill the best books and serve the quintessence of wisdom. But he that cannot have sages in service should have them for his friends.

Knowledge is portrayed as essential for a meaningful existence, with real-life inseparable from pursuing and acquiring knowledge. Here, the author underscores the value of surrounding oneself with intellectual champions and wise advisors, highlighting the privilege and wisdom in seeking guidance from those who excel in knowledge and insight. Indeed, having access to the wisdom of intellectuals serves as a shield against ignorance and a source of solutions to complex problems. In addition, employing those more intelligent than yourself as "servants" could be seen as a novel form of supremacy since it elevates one's status and enhances the quality of life.

The text emphasizes the efficiency and cleverness in leveraging the expertise of others to gain wisdom. Essentially, you acquire knowledge through the counsel of many as a form of study rather than via the more burdensome route of intense formal study yourself. By using the words of wise men, you will gain a reputation for wisdom. Whether in service or friendship, ministering spirits are depicted as invaluable assets, distilling the essence of wisdom from the best books and serving it to those in need.

REFLECTIONS

- Consider the idea of leveraging the expertise of others to overcome challenges and navigate complexities in life. Have there been instances where you sought guidance or assistance from individuals who were experts in their respective fields? How did their insights and advice contribute to finding solutions or achieving success?

- Explore the notion of learning from others without formal study. Have you gained valuable knowledge or wisdom through informal conversations, mentorship, or collaborative efforts? Reflect on the role of informal learning experiences in your personal and professional development.

- Reflect on the importance of humility in seeking guidance from others who may possess more excellent knowledge or expertise. How do you approach situations where you recognize the need for assistance or guidance from individuals who are more knowledgeable than yourself?

- Consider the role of reciprocity in relationships with intellectual peers and mentors. Have you ever had the opportunity to share your insights and knowledge with others in a mentoring or teaching capacity? How do you contribute to the collective wisdom and growth of your social or professional networks?

- Reflect on the value of friendship with individuals who possess wisdom and insight. How do these friendships enrich your life and contribute to your personal growth and development? Consider the qualities you admire in these individuals and how they inspire you to cultivate wisdom in your own life.

- Explore becoming a conduit for knowledge and wisdom in your personal and professional spheres. How can you leverage your experiences and insights to support and uplift others toward wisdom and personal fulfillment?

ACKNOWLEDGE AND MEND WHAT'S UNKNOWN

BY MAKING WISE MINDS YOUR OWN,

CLEVERNESS LIES IN LEARNING WIDE,

YOU'LL GAIN MUCH THROUGH MANY A GUIDE.

My Dearest Friend,

In the intricate dance of power and politics, wisdom reigns supreme. As I have often espoused in my works, *The Art of Wisdom* is not merely a virtue to be admired but a crucial tool for those who seek to navigate the treacherous waters of governance. Allow me to elucidate further on the Machiavellian interpretation of the usefulness of this art.

In pursuing and maintaining power, a ruler must possess intellectual prowess and a keen understanding of human nature. It is this wisdom that enables one to discern the motives and intentions of others, to anticipate potential obstacles, and to adapt strategies accordingly. Prudence, my dear friend, is the cornerstone of effective leadership.

Moreover, wisdom extends beyond mere intellect to encompass an intelligent understanding of power dynamics. A ruler must project an image of sagacity and prudence to gain the trust and loyalty of their subjects. However, behind this facade lies a strategic mind willing to employ deception and manipulation to achieve political objectives.

Wisdom dictates keeping friends and enemies close in relationships and alliances. Cultivating alliances with those with knowledge and expertise is essential, leveraging their intellect to advance one's political agenda. These "ministering spirits," as I have termed them, are invaluable assets in pursuing power.

However, let us remember the moral responsibilities of leadership. While wisdom may necessitate deception and manipulation, it also demands virtuous governance. A wise ruler must strike a delicate balance between pragmatism and morality, using their wisdom not only to attain power but also to govern wisely and justly for the benefit of their subjects.

In conclusion, my dear friend, wisdom is indispensable to those seeking to wield power effectively. It is a tool for achieving and maintaining power, essential for navigating the complexities of politics and securing long-term success. Let us, therefore, embrace wisdom as our guiding light in the tumultuous world of governance.

Yours in wisdom and prudence,

Niccolò Machiavelli

STRATEGIES

Identify and Exploit Power Dynamics: Identify individuals with significant influence or power within your social, professional, or political sphere. Cultivate relationships with these individuals by offering flattery, loyalty, or valuable services in exchange for their mentorship or support.

Create a Persona of Wisdom and Knowledge: Craft a persona of wisdom, intelligence, and sophistication to attract the attention and admiration of intellectual elites. Use rhetoric, charisma, and persuasion to portray yourself as a knowledgeable and insightful individual worthy of their attention and respect.

Use Information as Currency: Leverage information as a form of currency to gain favor with influential individuals. Collect valuable insights, insider knowledge, or sensitive information that can be used to demonstrate your value to those in power.

Pit Competitors Against Each Other: Exploit rivalries and conflicts among intellectual elites to your advantage. Stir dissent, sow discord, or manipulate interpersonal dynamics to weaken competitors and position yourself as a valuable ally or confidant.

Offer Indirect Assistance and Support: Provide indirect assistance and support to influential individuals without appearing overtly subservient or obsequious. Use subtle gestures, favors, or acts of kindness to ingratiate yourself with those in power subtly.

Play on Ego and Vanity: Appeal to the ego and vanity of intellectual elites by praising their intellect, accomplishments, or influence. Stroke their ego, flatter their sense of superiority, and make them feel valued and respected in your presence.

Maintain a Facade of Loyalty and Devotion: Project an image of unwavering loyalty and devotion to those in power while secretly pursuing your agenda and interests. Use deception, manipulation, and strategic ambiguity to conceal your intentions and motives.

GATHER INSIGHTS, SECRETS, AND MORE,

TO CHOOSE THE RIGHT PATH AND OPEN DOORS,

MANIPULATE DYNAMICS TO AUGMENT YOUR MIGHT,

AND POSITION YOURSELF IN THE BEST LIGHT.

16 - KNOWLEDGE AND GOOD INTENTIONS

Knowledge and Good Intentions together ensure the continuance of success. A fine intellect wedded to a wicked will was always an unnatural monster. A wicked will envenoms all excellences: helped by knowledge, it only ruins with greater subtlety. 'Tis a miserable superiority that only results in ruin. Knowledge without sense is double folly.

racián emphasizes the symbiotic relationship between intellect and moral character in achieving sustained success and avoiding moral pitfalls.

The text underscores the notion that possessing knowledge alone is insufficient for achieving lasting success. Instead, when knowledge is coupled with good intentions, it is a powerful force for driving positive outcomes. This pairing ensures that the actions taken are guided by ethical principles and a genuine desire to do good.

Conversely, the text warns against the dangers of possessing a fine intellect but harboring a wicked will. Such a combination is likened to an unnatural monster, suggesting that intellect divorced from moral integrity leads to destructive behavior. A wicked will can corrupt and undermine all forms of excellence, and when coupled with knowledge, it only amplifies its destructive potential with greater subtlety.

The text suggests that any form of superiority achieved through knowledge and intellect alone is ultimately hollow and miserable if it leads to ruin. True success and fulfillment can only be attained when good intentions and moral integrity temper knowledge.

Furthermore, it emphasizes the folly of possessing knowledge without sense or moral discernment. In such cases, knowledge becomes a liability rather than an asset, leading to misguided actions and detrimental outcomes.

The text highlights the importance of aligning knowledge with good intentions to ensure individuals' and society's continued success and well-being. It serves as a reminder that intellect should be guided by moral principles and used for the betterment of oneself and others rather than for self-serving or destructive purposes.

REFLECTIONS

- Reflect on when you witnessed someone with considerable knowledge or intellect misuse their abilities due to a lack of good intentions. How did this experience shape your understanding of aligning knowledge with moral integrity?

- Consider a situation where you were faced with a decision that required both knowledge and good intentions. How did you navigate this situation? What factors influenced your decision-making process, and what were the outcomes?

- Explore the concept of "miserable superiority" described in the prompt. Have you ever encountered individuals who exhibited superior knowledge or intellect but lacked moral integrity? How did their actions ultimately lead to ruin?

- Reflect on the idea of "knowledge without sense" being double folly. Can you think of instances where someone possessed a wealth of knowledge but lacked practical wisdom or common sense? How did this impact their ability to achieve success or make sound decisions?

- Consider your approach to acquiring knowledge and fostering good intentions. How do you ensure that a commitment to ethical principles and moral integrity accompanies your pursuit of knowledge? How do you integrate these aspects into your personal and professional life?

- Consider examples from history or literature where characters or individuals exemplified the ideal combination of knowledge and good intentions. What lessons can be drawn from these examples, and how can they be applied to contemporary contexts?

- Reflect on the broader implications of the prompt for society as a whole. How does aligning knowledge and good intentions contribute to the well-being and progress of communities and societies? What challenges arise when these two elements are not in harmony, and how can they be addressed?

UNGUARDED INTENTIONS CAN POISON DEEDS AND CORRUPT THE MIND,

LEAVING CHAOS AND DESTRUCTION BEHIND.

WHEN KNOWLEDGE SERVES ONLY TO MISLEAD

A SORRY POSITION RESULTS, INDEED.

My Dearest Reader,

Allow me to reflect on the intertwining concepts of knowledge and good intentions. In our pursuit of greatness and success, we often attribute immense value to knowledge, and rightly so. However, it is crucial to recognize that knowledge alone cannot guarantee our triumph. No, my friend, the marriage of knowledge with virtuous intentions ensures our enduring success. For you see, a fine intellect, when wedded to a wicked will, becomes an unnatural monster—a force capable of wreaking havoc and causing irreparable harm.

Indeed, a wicked will has the insidious power to corrupt all other virtues and excellences, rendering them ineffectual and even destructive. Even the most profound knowledge, when wielded by evil intentions, serves only to magnify the extent of the harm inflicted upon others. Thus, it is folly to believe that intellect alone can secure our triumph if it is divorced from moral integrity.

Furthermore, my dear friend, I must caution against pursuing superiority solely based on intellect without considering ethical principles. Such a pursuit, lacking moral sensibility, inevitably leads to ruin rather than genuine success. True greatness, you see, lies not merely in the realm of intellect but also in the domain of character and ethical conduct.

Therefore, let us strive to cultivate both our intellect and our moral compass in equal measure. Let us harness the power of knowledge with virtuous intentions, for it is in the harmonious fusion of these two elements that we find the path to enduring success and greatness.

Yours in wisdom and discernment,

Niccolò Machiavelli

STRATEGIES

Cultivate Knowledge: Dedicate yourself to acquiring knowledge in various fields, encompassing practical skills and theoretical understanding.

Develop Good Intentions: Cultivate virtuous intentions and ethical principles to guide your actions and decisions.

Integrate Knowledge and Good Intentions: Recognize the synergy between knowledge and virtuous intentions, understanding that they complement each other to ensure success.

Avoid a Wicked Will: Guard against using knowledge for malicious purposes, as it ultimately leads to ruin.

Strive for Intellectual and Moral Excellence: Pursue intellectual prowess and moral integrity, both essential to greatness.

Balance Intellect and Virtue: Maintain a delicate balance between intellect and virtue, understanding that neither can thrive in isolation.

Utilize Knowledge Ethically: Apply your knowledge ethically and responsibly, ensuring it serves the greater good rather than selfish interests.

Seek Wisdom: Surround yourself with wise mentors and advisors who can impart valuable knowledge and ethical guidance.

Constantly Improve: Strive for continuous improvement in knowledge and virtue, recognizing that greatness is an ongoing pursuit.

Exercise Caution: Exercise caution and discernment in pursuing knowledge, avoiding the allure of power and dominance at the expense of ethical principles.

BEWARE THE ALLURE OF A WICKED WILL,

FOR SECURE POWER DEMANDS ACCRUING GOODWILL.

WICKEDNESS IS NOT THE WAY -

UNMITIGATED EVIL UNDERMINES AND LEADS YOU ASTRAY.

17 - VARY THE MODE OF ACTION

Vary the Mode of Action; sometimes the same way, to distract attention, especially if there is a rival. Only sometimes, from the first impulse, they will soon recognize the uniformity and, by anticipating, frustrate your designs. It is easy to kill a bird on the wing that flies straight, not so one that twists. Nor always act on second thoughts: they can discern the plan the second time. The enemy is on the watch, and great skill is required to circumvent him. The gamester needs to play the card the opponent expects, which is still less than he wants.

Strategic maneuvering and deception are essential for navigating the complexities of human interaction and competition. At its core, the aphorism emphasizes the importance of unpredictability and versatility in one's actions to outwit adversaries and maintain an edge in confrontational situations. The notion of varying the mode of action underscores the need to avoid falling into predictable patterns of behavior or decision-making. By adopting different approaches and tactics, individuals can effectively distract attention from their true intentions and keep adversaries balanced.

Furthermore, these words highlight the perils of acting solely on the first impulse or consistently relying on the same strategies. Such tendencies render one's actions predictable and make them vulnerable to exploitation by astute opponents. Instead, strategic thinkers recognize the  importance of judiciously timing their actions and avoiding rash decisions that may backfire.

Moreover, the aphorism warns against complacency and emphasizes continual vigilance in dealing with adversaries. The enemy is ever watchful, seeking to anticipate and thwart one's designs. Therefore, great skill and cunning are required to circumvent their defenses and achieve one's objectives.

REFLECTIONS

- Reflect on when you faced a challenging situation where your actions were predictable. How did the predictability affect the outcome, and what lessons did you learn from that experience?

- Consider a recent decision you made based on impulse. Reflect on whether acting impulsively served your best interests or if it led to unforeseen consequences. How might you approach similar situations differently in the future?

- Consider a rival or competitor in work, relationships, or personal endeavors. How do you currently interact with this rival, and are there patterns in your behavior that they may have begun to anticipate? How could you vary your approach to keep them off balance?

- Reflect on a time when you hesitated to take action due to second thoughts or indecision. How did this hesitation impact the situation, and what could you have done differently to maintain the upper hand?

- Consider the concept of strategic deception and misdirection. Reflect on whether you have ever employed such tactics to gain an advantage in a competitive situation and how effective they were in achieving your desired outcome.

- Consider the qualities of a skilled gamester who never plays the expected card. How might you apply this mindset to your decision-making and strategic planning in various areas?

- Reflect on the role of observation and awareness in circumventing adversaries. How attuned are you to the behaviors and intentions of others, and how might you improve your ability to anticipate their moves and counteract them effectively?

A TWIST AND TURN, A SUBTLE BEND,

MAKES OUR MOVES HARDER COMPREHEND.

KEEP YOUR FOES GUESSING AND ON EDGE.

BY MOVING STRATEGICALLY, YOU STAY AHEAD.

My Dear Friend,

I trust this message finds you well and in good spirits. I write to you today with advice that I believe will serve you well in your endeavors: "Vary the Mode of Action."

Predictability is a weakness in the intricate dance of politics and power, and unpredictability is a strength to be cultivated. By changing your tactics and strategies frequently, you keep your adversaries guessing and unable to anticipate your next move. This element of surprise can be a potent weapon in your arsenal, allowing you to maintain the upper hand and achieve your objectives more efficiently.

Consider the analogy I employ of the bird on the wing: it is far easier to capture a bird that flies straight and true than one that twists and turns unpredictably. Similarly, by avoiding patterns of behavior and refusing to adhere to a fixed course of action, you create confusion and uncertainty among your rivals, making it difficult for them to formulate effective countermeasures against you.

Furthermore, I caution against relying solely on first impulses or second thoughts. Both can be easily discerned and exploited by observant opponents. Instead, I urge you to adopt a calculated and deliberate approach, carefully considering each action to maximize its strategic impact.

In conclusion, my friend, remember that success in the game of politics requires cunning, adaptability, and strategic thinking. By varying your mode of action and keeping your adversaries off balance, you can confidently navigate the treacherous waters of power and achieve your goals more efficiently.

Yours faithfully,

Niccolò Machiavelli

STRATEGIES

Avoid relying solely on first impulses: Consider your actions carefully and avoid acting impulsively, as opponents can easily exploit predictable behavior.

Beware of second thoughts: Be cautious of overthinking or hesitating, as this can also make your intentions and strategies transparent to others.

Cultivate a reputation for cunning: Project an image of strategic thinking and cleverness to keep adversaries on their toes and maintain an aura of mystery and intrigue.

Create confusion and uncertainty: Use ambiguity and misdirection to your advantage, making it difficult for opponents to discern your true intentions or motives.

Utilize strategic deception: Employ tactics such as feints, misdirection, and deception to manipulate perceptions and mislead adversaries about your objectives.

Maintain the element of surprise: Keep adversaries off balance by introducing unexpected twists or changes in your plans, catching them off guard and forcing them to react defensively.

Anticipate countermeasures: Stay one step ahead of opponents by anticipating their likely responses and preparing counter-strategies to neutralize or mitigate their effectiveness.

Adapt to changing circumstances: Be flexible and adaptable in your approach, adjusting your strategies to navigate shifting political or social dynamics.

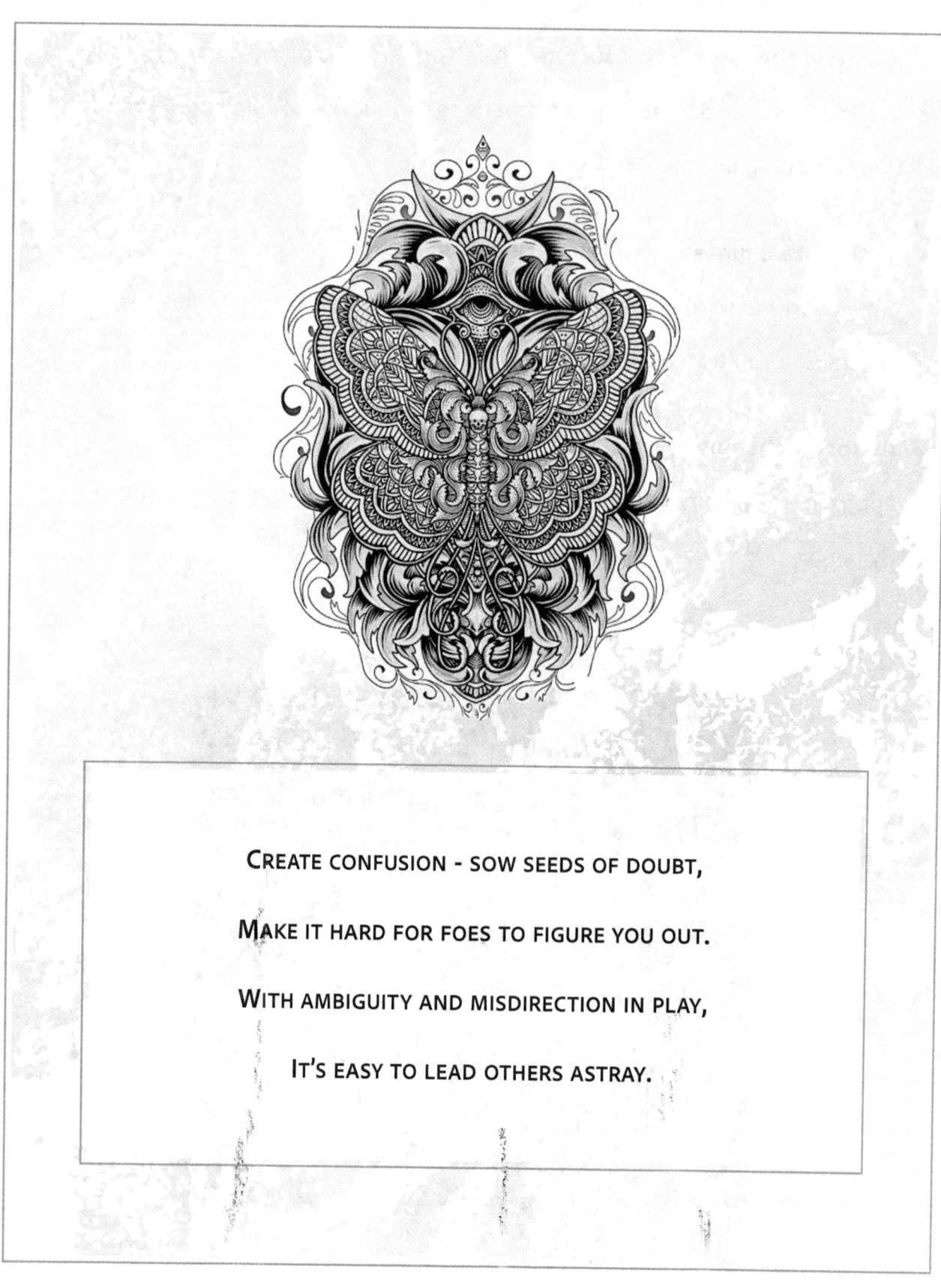

CREATE CONFUSION - SOW SEEDS OF DOUBT,

MAKE IT HARD FOR FOES TO FIGURE YOU OUT.

WITH AMBIGUITY AND MISDIRECTION IN PLAY,

IT'S EASY TO LEAD OTHERS ASTRAY.

18 - APPLICATION AND ABILITY

Application and Ability | There is no attaining eminence without both; where they unite, there is the greatest eminence. Mediocrity obtains more with application than superiority without it. Work is the price that is paid for reputation. What costs little is little worth. Even for the highest posts, it is only in some cases that application is wanted, rarely the talent. To prefer moderate success in great things than eminence in a humble post has the excuse of a generous mind, but not so to be content with humble mediocrity when you could shine among the highest. Thus, nature and art are needed, and application sets them the seal.

These words encapsulate the essential components necessary for achieving greatness. According to Gracián, eminence cannot be attained without the harmonious combination of application and ability. When these two elements converge, they give rise to the pinnacle of excellence.

In Gracián's view, mediocrity often prevails when there is diligent application, even without superior talent. This underscores the importance of hard work and dedication in pursuing success. Indeed, work is portrayed as the currency exchanged for reputation, implying that proper recognition is earned through sustained effort and diligence.

Furthermore, Gracián suggests that the value of one's achievements is proportional to the effort invested. Anything obtained with minimal exertion is deemed worthless, reinforcing that significant accomplishments require substantial commitment and sacrifice.

Gracián contrasts settling for moderate success in lofty endeavors with accepting eminence in humble positions. While the former may be attributed to a generous disposition, the latter reflects a lack of ambition and self-awareness. He posits that true fulfillment lies in striving for greatness and maximizing one's potential rather than resigning to a state of humble mediocrity.

REFLECTIONS

- Consider Gracián's assertion that mediocrity often prevails with diligent application, even without superior talent. Do you agree or disagree with this perspective based on your experiences or observations?

- Evaluate your approach to work and achievement. Are you more inclined to prioritize application, ability, or a balance of both? How has this influenced your successes and failures?

- Consider Gracián's distinction between settling for moderate success in grand endeavors versus embracing eminence in humble roles. Reflect on your ambitions and aspirations—are you content with your current trajectory, or do you aspire to reach greater heights?

- Explore the role of ambition and self-awareness in your pursuit of success. Are there areas where you may be selling yourself short or underestimating your potential? How can you cultivate a mindset that encourages continuous growth and achievement?

- Reflect on Gracián's assertion that true fulfillment lies in striving for greatness and maximizing one's potential. How does this idea resonate with your values and aspirations? What steps can you take to align your actions with this philosophy?

- Consider the significance of balancing natural talent with dedicated effort in pursuing goals. How can you leverage your strengths while investing in continuous learning and skill development?

- Reflect on the concept of work as the price paid for reputation. How does this perspective influence your attitude toward hard work and perseverance? What motivates you to persist in the face of challenges and setbacks?

To remain content with modest fame,

When you could soar in a loftier aim,

Is to deny your true potential's call,

And let mediocrity befall.

My Dear Friend,

In contemplating the aphorism "Application and Ability," we are confronted with a profound truth that resonates deeply with the principles of statecraft and governance. Please permit me to expound upon this notion and elucidate its implications for those who aspire to wield power and influence in the tumultuous arena of politics.

First, let us acknowledge the indispensable role of application and ability in pursuing eminence. While natural talent and intellect may bestow certain advantages upon individuals, the relentless application of these gifts distinguishes the eminent from the mediocre. As you know, the path to greatness is paved with innate talent and the sweat and toil of tireless endeavor.

Indeed, reputation is the currency of politics and is earned through diligently applying one's abilities. Reputation serves as a measure of one's power and influence, shaping perceptions and facilitating alliances. Therefore, it behooves us to invest considerable effort in cultivating and safeguarding our reputation, for it is the bedrock upon which our political fortunes rest.

Furthermore, I caution against the perils of complacency and mediocrity. Those who aspire to greatness must eschew the comforts of the status quo and embrace the audacity of ambition. Mediocrity, my friend, is the enemy of eminence, and those who settle for humble mediocrity squander the opportunity to ascend to the highest echelons of power and influence.

In conclusion, heed the wisdom encapsulated in the aphorism "Application and Ability." By marrying the relentless application of our talents with the strategic deployment of our abilities, we may aspire to achieve greatness and leave an indelible mark upon the annals of history.

Yours faithfully,

Niccolò Machiavelli

STRATEGIES

Strategic Application of Talent: Recognize the importance of both innate ability and diligent application. Invest effort in honing natural talents while committing to disciplined and persistent work habits.

Building Reputation: Understand that reputation is a valuable asset in politics. Focus on cultivating a positive reputation through consistent performance and demonstrating competence in various endeavors.

Continuous Improvement: Embrace a mindset of continuous improvement and growth. Never become complacent with existing abilities but constantly seek to expand knowledge and skills through learning and practice.

Ambition and Audacity: Avoid settling for mediocrity or accepting humble positions when more significant opportunities for success and influence are within reach. Cultivate ambition and audacity in pursuing goals and aspirations.

Strategic Alliances: Leverage reputation and abilities to forge strategic alliances and partnerships. Collaborate with individuals who complement your skills and contribute to mutual success.

Strategic Positioning: Strategically position yourself to capitalize on opportunities for advancement and success. Be proactive in seeking out favorable circumstances and positioning yourself for favorable outcomes.

Long-Term Vision: Maintain a long-term perspective and avoid short-sighted decisions that may compromise prospects. Plan and strategize to achieve sustained success and longevity in your endeavors.

Adaptability: Recognize the importance of adaptability in navigating changing circumstances and challenges. Be prepared to adjust strategies and tactics as needed to overcome obstacles and seize opportunities.

Strategic Communication: Effectively communicate your abilities and achievements to others, strategically managing perceptions to enhance reputation and influence. Use language and rhetoric to convey competence and authority in your field.

AMBITION AND AUDACITY ARE FUEL FOR THE FIRE.

DON'T SETTLE FOR LESS, WHEN YOU CAN GO HIGHER.

REJECT MEDIOCRITY, REACH FOR THE SKY,

LET AMBITION AND AUDACITY BE YOUR BATTLE CRY.

19 - AROUSE NO EXAGGERATED EXPECTATIONS ON ENTERING

Arouse No Exaggerated Expectations on Entering | It is the usual bad luck of all celebrities not to fulfill the expectations beforehand formed of them afterward. The real can never equal the imagined, for it is easy to form ideals but very difficult to realize them. Imagination weds Hope and gives birth to much more than things are in themselves. However great the excellences, they never suffice to fulfill expectations, and as men find themselves disappointed with their unreasonable expectations, they are more ready to be disillusioned than to admire. Hope is a great falsifier of truth; let skill guard against this by ensuring that fruition exceeds desire. A few creditable attempts at the beginning are sufficient to arouse curiosity without pledging one to the final object. It is better that reality should surpass the design and is better than was thought. This rule does not apply to the wicked, for the same exaggeration is an excellent aid to them; they are defeated amid general applause, and what seemed at first extreme ruin comes to be thought quite bearable.

here is a delicate balance between perception and reality - particularly in celebrity and achievement. So, this text warns against the pitfalls of inflating expectations beyond what reality can fulfill and advocates for managing perceptions skillfully to avoid disappointment. The modern world is obsessed with fame and celebrity, and individuals often find themselves burdened with lofty expectations placed upon them by others. However, an imagined ideal created in their minds is far more glorious than what reality can

deliver, leading to inevitable disappointment when reality fails to measure up.

Gracián stresses the importance of adeptly managing expectations to prevent disillusionment. He cautions against making grand promises, instead recommending a measured approach with modest yet credible initial attempts. While this principle suits those pursuing excellence, the wicked may exploit exaggerated expectations to mask failure and evade judgment.

REFLECTIONS

- Reflect on a time when you or someone you know experienced disappointment due to exaggerated expectations. How did it affect your perception of the situation or individual involved?

- Consider a situation where you successfully managed expectations to avoid disappointment or dissatisfaction. What strategies did you employ, and what were the outcomes?

- Think about a goal or aspiration you have. How do you perceive the path to achieving it, and are there any unrealistic expectations you must address?

- Explore the role of hope and imagination in shaping your expectations. How do these factors influence your perception of reality, and how can you manage them more effectively?

- Consider Gracián's advice in the context of personal or professional relationships. How can you ensure that your actions and communication align with realistic expectations?

- Reflect on the concept of skillfully balancing ambition and humility. How can you set meaningful goals without succumbing to the pressure of exaggerated expectations?

- Explore instances in history or literature where individuals or societies faced the consequences of inflated expectations. What lessons can be learned from these examples?

- Consider the impact of social media and popular culture on shaping societal expectations. How do these platforms contribute to the proliferation of exaggerated ideals, and how can individuals mitigate their influence?

- Reflect on the notion of "fruition exceeding desire." Have there been moments in your life where reality positively surpassed your expectations? How did it feel, and what lessons did you learn?

AROUSE NO EXAGGERATED EXPECTATIONS, THEY SAY,

BETTER TO EXCEED, THAN FALL AWAY.

FOR IN THE END, IT'S NOT THE START,

BUT THE JOURNEY ITSELF, THAT SETS US APART.

My Dearest Confidant,

In the intricate dance of power and influence, one must tread carefully to avoid the pitfalls of inflated expectations. With this wisdom, I impart the strategic counsel encapsulated in the aphorism, "Arouse No Exaggerated Expectations on Entering."

As we both know, the road to greatness is often paved with the lofty ideals and grandiose imaginings of others. Yet, reality seldom aligns perfectly with the visions concocted by the vibrant imaginations of hopeful onlookers. Thus, it falls upon the astute practitioner of statecraft to temper the expectations of those around them lest they be trapped by the inevitable disillusionment that follows unfulfilled promises.

Celebrities and leaders alike are vulnerable to the perils of exaggerated expectations, for they are placed upon pedestals constructed from the lofty aspirations of admirers. Yet, as I have often observed, it is far more prudent to cultivate an air of mystery and intrigue, allowing curiosity to flourish without succumbing to the temptation of over-promising.

Indeed, the art of managing perceptions is delicate, requiring a skilled manipulator's deft hand. By carefully orchestrating the impressions we convey, we can ensure that reality exceeds the expectations of those around us, thus maintaining our strategic advantage in the ever-shifting landscape of power dynamics.

However, my dear friend, we must also remain vigilant to the potential machinations of the wicked, who may seek to exploit the very principle we employ for their nefarious ends. Let us not be deceived by the false promises of evil but instead remain steadfast in our commitment to truth and virtue.

In conclusion, remember that it is better to underpromise and overdeliver than to fall short of the grandiose expectations imposed upon us. May this counsel serve you well as you navigate the treacherous waters of ambition and intrigue?

Yours faithfully,

Niccolò Machiavelli

STRATEGIES

Cultivate an air of mystery and intrigue: Keep your intentions veiled to avoid arousing exaggerated expectations.

Manage perceptions carefully: Ensure that reality exceeds the expectations of others by underpromising and overdelivering.

Avoid overpromising: Temper the expectations of those around you to prevent disillusionment.

Use curiosity to your advantage: Foster interest and intrigue without committing to outcomes.

Be vigilant of the intentions of others: Guard against the potential exploitation of your actions by the unscrupulous.

Maintain a strategic advantage: Navigate the complex power dynamics with skill and foresight.

Embrace the art of manipulation: Use perception management to control the narrative and shape outcomes.

Exercise discretion in communication: Share information selectively to maintain an aura of mystery and control.

Balance ambition with prudence: Strive for greatness while avoiding the pitfalls of excessive expectation.

Prioritize reality over perception: Ensure your actions and achievements align with your project image.

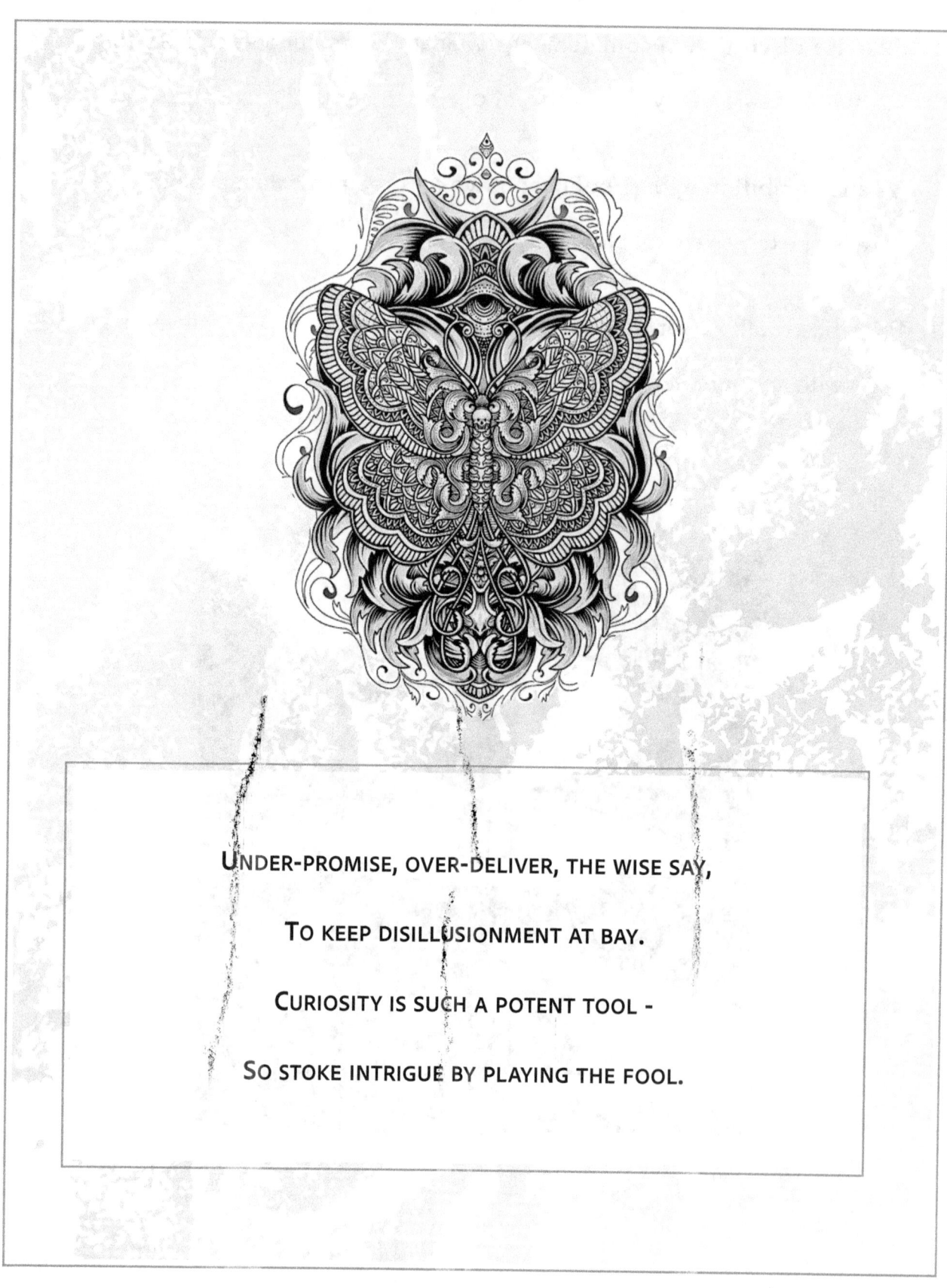

Under-promise, over-deliver, the wise say,

To keep disillusionment at bay.

Curiosity is such a potent tool -

So stoke intrigue by playing the fool.

20 - A MAN OF THE AGE

A Man of the Age | The rarest individuals depend on their age. Only some people find the age they deserve; even when they find it, they only sometimes know how to utilize it. Some men have been worthy of a better century, for every species of good does not always triumph. Things have their period; even excellences are subject to fashion. The sage has one advantage: he is immortal. If this is not his century, many others will be.

his text encapsulates the profound idea that individuals are deeply intertwined with the historical context in which they exist. According to Gracián, the rarest individuals are ideally suited to their era, harnessing the spirit of their time to achieve greatness.

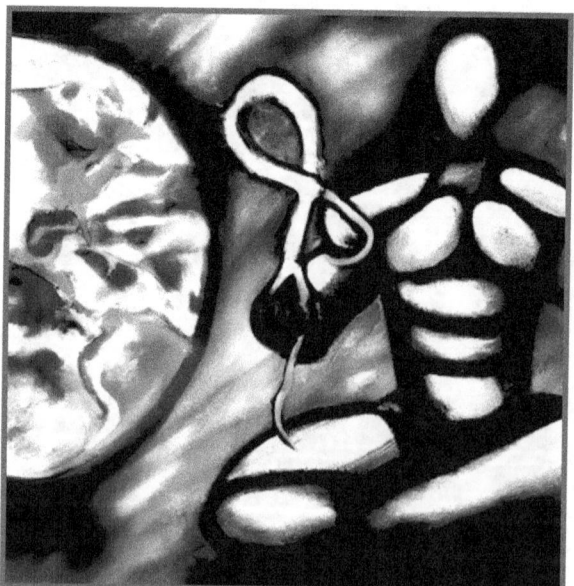

However, not everyone finds themselves in the age they deserve, and even when they do, they may struggle to capitalize on their opportunities fully.

Throughout history, there have been individuals whose virtues and talents transcended the limitations

of their time, shining brightly amidst the prevailing darkness. Conversely, there have been those who, despite their potential, found themselves overshadowed by their age's prevailing trends and ideologies. Gracián suggests that the alignment between an individual and their era is crucial for realizing one's full potential and leaving a lasting impact on the world.

Nevertheless, Gracián offers hope to those who feel out of place in their own time. He suggests that the sage, the truly wise and enlightened individual, possesses an inherent immortality that transcends the constraints of any single era. While they may not find recognition and appreciation in their century, the sage's wisdom will endure, resonating across generations and inspiring future generations.

REFLECTIONS

- Reflect on a time when you felt deeply connected to the spirit of your era. What aspects of the contemporary culture, values, or trends resonated with you? How did you leverage this alignment to achieve your goals or make a positive impact?

- Consider instances when you felt out of sync with your time's prevailing attitudes or norms. How did you navigate this sense of dissonance? Did you find ways to adapt and thrive within your environment, or did you seek to challenge and reshape the prevailing zeitgeist?

- Explore the concept of immortality as discussed in Gracián's aphorism. What does it mean to leave a lasting legacy beyond one's era? Reflect on individuals or historical figures who have achieved enduring significance despite the changing tides of history.

- Contemplate the idea of excellence being subject to fashion. How do societal values and standards of greatness evolve? Consider examples of virtues or talents that were once revered but are now considered outdated or irrelevant, and vice versa.

- Reflect on your aspirations and ambitions in light of Gracián's aphorism. How do you perceive your relationship to the age in which you live? Do you feel aligned with the prevailing trends and values, or do you feel disconnected? How might you leverage your unique talents and virtues to navigate and thrive within your era?

WISDOM ALONE HAS INFINITE GLEAM,

FOR IN EVERY ERA, IT REIGNS SUPREME.

IF THIS ERA DOES NOT FAVOR YOUR FATE,

DESPAIR NOT FOR ANOTHER AWAITS.

———

My Dear Friend,

In contemplating Baltasar Gracián's aphorism on being a "Man of the Age," I cannot help but reflect on the profound wisdom it holds for leaders like yourself. It speaks to the essence of political acumen and the art of governance that I have long championed.

To be a true "Man of the Age" is to possess an acute awareness of our time's currents and skillfully maneuver within them. Just as a seasoned sailor must understand the winds and tides to navigate the seas, so must a prudent leader comprehend our era's prevailing trends, values, and power dynamics to maintain their influence and achieve their aims.

For you, my friend, this means embracing the spirit of our age with discernment and adaptability. It requires a keen eye for opportunity and a readiness to seize upon the circumstances presented by our ever-changing world. While some may lament not living in a more promising era, I urge you to recognize that true greatness lies not in longing for different times but in making the most of the opportunities afforded us here and now.

Indeed, as Gracián astutely observes, every era has its peculiarities and challenges, and it is our task to rise to the occasion and leave our mark upon history. Whether it be through cunning diplomacy, strategic alliances, or bold action, I have every confidence that you possess the wit and resourcefulness to navigate the complexities of our age and emerge

triumphant.

Remember, my friend, that while the times may change, the principles of

statecraft remain constant. By embodying the virtues of adaptability,

pragmatism, and opportunism, you will undoubtedly cement your place as

a true "Man of the Age."

Yours faithfully,

Niccolò Machiavelli

STRATEGIES

Study the Current Age: Keep a finger on the pulse of the times, understanding the prevailing trends, values, and power dynamics.

Adaptability: Be flexible and adaptable in your approach, ready to adjust your strategies and tactics as circumstances change.

Opportunism: Seize upon the opportunities presented by the current age, leveraging them to your advantage whenever possible.

Discernment: Exercise discernment in your actions, distinguishing between fleeting fads and enduring principles and aligning yourself with the latter.

Strategic Alliances: Forge alliances and partnerships with individuals or groups that wield influence in the current age, leveraging their support to further your goals.

Bold Action: Be willing to take bold and decisive action when necessary, capitalizing on moments of opportunity to advance your agenda.

Pragmatism: Embrace pragmatism in decision-making, prioritizing practical considerations over ideological or moral concerns.

Long-Term Vision: Maintain a long-term perspective, understanding that success in the current age often requires patience, perseverance, and a strategic vision for the future.

Exploit Weaknesses: Identify and exploit the weaknesses of your rivals or adversaries, capitalizing on any vulnerabilities to weaken their position and strengthen your own.

Cunning Diplomacy: Engage in cunning diplomacy, using tact, diplomacy, and manipulation to navigate the complexities of the current age and advance your interests.

With fate and strategy in hand,

We navigate this shifting land.

Study the age, its ebb and flow,

To choose the best way to go.

Journal

MY INDEX

TOPIC	PAGE(S)

MY INDEX

TOPIC	PAGE(S)